Telling Your Story:
A Narrative Approach to Public Speaking

Philadelphia Press is an eco-friendly, environmentally concious company.
We strive to keep our carbon footprint to an absolute minimum,
and to deliver non-paper products whenever possible.

All rights reserved. No part of this book may be reproduced or utilized in any form or by any means,
electronic or mechanical, including photocopying and recording, or by any information storage
and retrieval system without written permission from the publisher.

Books may be purchased for educational purposes.

For information, please call or write:

(888) 851-3367

Philadelphia Press
7715 Crittenden St. #390
Philadelphia, PA 19118

Web site: wwwphiladelphiapress.com.
Email: info@philadelphiapress.com

ISBN 978-0-9974030-0-8

Printed in the United States of America

Table of Contents

Why Is It Important to Tell Your Story?.. vii

Our Stories.. 1
    Explanation of Narrative Components:.. 7

Chapter One: Backstage... 23
    Models of Communication... 23
    Differences between Public Speaking and Casual Conversation............................ 29

Chapter Two: What's Your Story?.. 31
    It Starts with You... 31
    Audience Analysis... 35
    Your General and Specific Purpose.. 36
    Overall Questions to Consider when Selecting a Topic.. 37

Chapter Three: A Tale of Three Speeches... 43
    Narrative Speech... 43
    Informative Speech.. 51
    Persuasive Speech... 61

Chapter Four: Getting Your Story Straight... 73
    Sources.. 73
    Logic, Reasoning, Evidence, and Ethics.. 78

Chapter Five: The Plot Thickens... 109
    Developing Your Central Idea and Main Points... 109
    Strategies for Organizing Your Speech.. 111
    Constructing and Using an Outline... 112

Chapter Six: Show & Tell 117
    Nonverbal Communication and Delivery 117
    Incorporating Presentation Aids 118

Chapter Seven: Assignments 121
    Folk Tale Speech 123
    Speech of Demonstration 127
    Speech of Causality 131
    Speech of Analysis 135
    Proposition of Fact 139
    Proposition of Value 143
    Proposition of Policy 147

Chapter Eight: Tricks of the Trade 151
    Practicing Effectively 151
    Helpful Hints 154

Chapter Nine: Relaxing into Your Story:
    How to use Meditation to Control Speech Anxiety 155
    Definition of Meditation 156
    Why Meditate? 157
    How to Meditate 159
    Procedure 164
    Optimal States of Meditation and Performance 166
    References 167

Appendix A: Analysis of Folktales 169
    The Girl without Hands 174
    Explanation of Narrative Components: 179

Appendix B: Analysis of The Moth 181
    A Very Dangerous Person 181

Appendix C: Analysis of TED.com 185
    Informative TED Talks 185
    Persuasive TED Talks 205

Foreword

Why Is It Important to Tell Your Story?

Imagine that you're about to be interviewed for the job of your dreams. You've worked long and hard in school, taken low-paying jobs to get through college and to pay for car insurance, and you still barely have enough left over to feed yourself and go out occasionally. But now you're sitting in the lobby of a massive professional building and mentally preparing yourself to get in the elevator that will take you to what may be the first big break of your career. Someone must have liked your résumé; otherwise, you wouldn't be here for the interview. They know you have decent grades, did some volunteer work, and have completed plenty of internship and entry level experience in the industry, so what are "they" looking for? What's the difference between success and failure in this case? How can you "seal the deal" and pull yourself out of the uncertainty and financial instability that's plagued your professional life thus far?

The answer to this question is disarmingly simple: a story. A résumé is an impersonal collection of facts about your career. Cover letters, letters of recommendation, samples of your work, and references provide more of a narrative, but still lack the personal context, spontaneity, and authenticity of a face-to-face encounter. Modern networking tools like Monster or LinkedIn are powerful and important, but physical presence is the oldest and most trusted form of interpersonal evaluation. And the best way to make a good impression is by telling your story. This doesn't mean you will shake hands at the interview, take a step back, and dramatically declare "Once upon a time...." Indeed, telling your story can be theatrical, but it can also be very subtle. First and foremost it requires your own "buy-in." In other words, do you have faith in the story you're telling? Does it feel authentic to you?

As you will learn in the pages that follow, "a story is nothing more than a series of events linked to one another to achieve a common end." In the case of our job interview above, the series of events might include courses you've taken, projects you've worked on, previous jobs you've had, volunteer work, hobbies, places you've visited, or anything else that brings your story to the logical common end (or conclusion) of getting the job. Also keep in mind that good stories, though perhaps resonating with reality, also take on a life of their own and need not be a precise history down to the last detail.

Always remember that the function of a story is to provide a structure to the disorganized mess of real life. This is why, even in informative and persuasive speeches, the use of narrative structure to frame the content of the speech can be very effective. For example, if as in

Susan Cain's TED talk (http://www.ted.com/talks/susan_cain_the_power_of_introverts), a story is used as a bracketing device in the introduction and conclusion, informative and/or persuasive content in the body of the speech becomes more relevant to the audience because we naturally connect with stories more than we do with numbers or facts that lack a context.

In the absence of stories, life is utterly without meaning. Cultures, religions, nations, cities, families, and individuals all construct meaning, and ultimately reality, through stories. Naturally, the power of that reality is determined by the power of the story, that is: how many people actually believe it and think it's important?

Returning to the example of our job interview, we might say that success is dependent upon convincing the interviewers that your story is more authentic and important than any other candidate's. However, the same might be said for the experience of presenting a business proposal to a group of investors, or going out on a first date, or taking the witness stand, or running for office, or mounting a global revolution, for that matter. Success or failure in these cases as in all human interaction is largely dependent upon the effectiveness of the story you tell.

OUR STORIES

The following stories have been written and performed as narrative speeches by the authors of this textbook. We intend for these to serve as examples of good storytelling and material for the analysis of narrative form. In Chapter Three: "A Tale of Three Speeches," you will learn about the format of the narrative speech and the components of effective storytelling. Critical to your success is the understanding that a narrative is *a series of events linked to one another to achieve a common end*. We will analyze the first story ("Sensei Chinen") together and identify the events, the common end (i.e., climax) and the other components of the narrative. You will analyze the remaining two stories according to the first example.

SENSEI CHINEN

Let me tell you a story.

The story I want to share with you explains why you're reading these words, why I've written them, why I've spoken them, and why I want to share the knowledge of using stories to improve your public communication skills. In short, this story explains why I decided to teach.

To begin this story we have to travel back in time to the year 1983. In 1983, R*eturn of the Jedi* was playing in movie theaters, television programs like *Cheers* and *Knight Rider* had made their debut, and the pervasive role of the Internet was all but absent from human consciousness.

In 1983, I was six years old and starting the first grade. At age six, I really wasn't a great student. In fact, I'm told I was really something of a selective mute who really didn't associate much with my classmates or talk to teachers. So my parents, trying to be conscientious, enrolled me at the local karate school hoping it would teach me some self-confidence and cure me of my shyness.

The name of the school was the Oakland Karate Academy and I still remember my first day very vividly. My mom held my hand as we walked in the front door of the dojo (karate school) one early Saturday morning. Strangely, I can recall wearing green corduroy pants and a shirt with green and brown stripes running across it. Walking in the front door, I was greeted with what seemed like a massive cave with wooden floors, mirror-lined walls, and a rack filled with all sorts of interesting weapons at the other side of the room. My Sensei (teacher) said hello and taught me a few basic things like how to stand at the "yoi" (ready) position, how to "rei" (bow) and how to sit in "seiza" (sitting) position on the insteps of my feet. I can remember that all of it seemed fascinating to me.

But the thing that would really leave an impression on me and set me off in a new direction (though I didn't know it at the time) came a few years later when I was ten years old and my mom dropped me and my friend Craig off at the dojo. As we walked in, we knew something was terribly wrong because the room was packed with adults wearing black belts that signified their high rank. Craig and I made our way through the crowd and were almost to the back of the room when the door opened again and a wave of silent electricity washed through the room. Suddenly, everyone in the dojo turned toward the door in unison and bowed, chanting "onegai shimasu" (please teach me). Sensei Chinen had entered the room.

It took me a while before I was able to peek around the adults and see who was at the center of all this attention. When I finally did manage to catch a glimpse, I observed an

Okinawan man not much taller than myself wearing a crisp, white uniform and a wornout black belt. He had a shaved head, a missing toe on his left foot, and large black pupils. There was no question to me then or now that he was by far the most intense and powerful presence that I'd ever experienced in my young life.

The evening carried on and it was loud, hot, and crowded. He barked commands in a deep, penetrating voice that were half in English and half in Japanese. Even without seeing him, I could sense his silent presence as he floated by, causing my muscles to tense and my hair to stand on end. There seemed to be a physical aura that surrounded him, warning of his power and intensity.

At one point, he lined everyone up in rows and told us all to lie down on our backs. We did this obediently and were further instructed to elevate our shoulders and legs off the ground and use our fists to pound on our bellies to condition the muscles. We all followed suit counting off painful blows in Japanese: ichi (one)… ni (two)… san (three)… shi (four)… go (five)… roku (six)… shichi (seven)… hachi (eight)… kyu (nine)… ju (ten)…. But as this went on, he began to go down each of the rows using his fists to test the strength of our stomach muscles himself. I was at the end of a long line of adult black-belts and became increasingly nervous as he continued down the row testing one student after another. My friend Craig was so shaken by this that he got up and left the room. (I later learned they had to call his parents to come pick him up early because he was so upset.) I was no less scared, but responded by staying put and just closing my eyes as he worked his way closer and closer, the strained sounds of pain and exertion filling the crowded space. Finally, he arrived at the man next to me. For whatever reason, the conditioning went especially hard on him. I could hear the dull thud of fists on the man's stomach as he howled in pain, crying out "onegai shimasu, Sensei, onegai shimasu, Sensei."

But when he finally got to me, he was much less violent and the trial was soon over. I was afraid, but for no reason.

A few weeks later both Craig and I received a letter in the mail from Sensei Chinen. In the letter he said he hoped he hadn't frightened me too much, but that he could also remember being scared of his Sensei when he was a little boy. It was short, but it carried a powerful message and inspiration that follows me to this day: A good teacher should be compassionate, but also intense, perhaps even a bit fierce and frightening, because the most important lessons we learn are hard-won and require courage. So as a student I learned the value of courage, and as a teacher I learned the value of intensity.

Thus, as you finish this course, I encourage you to go forward learning courageously and teaching intensely.

End.

	BREAKDOWN OF NARRATIVE COMPONENTS IN "SENSEI CHINEN"
Background 1	The story I want to share with you explains why you're reading these words, why I've written them, why I've spoken them, and why I want to share the knowledge of using stories to improve your public communication skills. In short, this story explains why I decided to teach.
Background 2	To begin this story we have to travel back in time to the year 1983. In 1983, *Return of the Jedi* was playing in movie theaters, television programs like *Cheers* and *Knight Rider* had made their debut, and the pervasive role of the Internet was all but absent from human consciousness
Background 3	In 1983, I was six years old and starting the first grade. At age six, I really wasn't a great student. In fact, I'm told I was really something of a selective mute who really didn't associate much with my classmates or talk to teachers. So my parents, trying to be conscientious, enrolled me at the local karate school hoping it would teach me some self-confidence and cure me of my shyness.
Transition 1	The name of the school was the Oakland Karate Academy and I still remember my first day very vividly.
Event 1	My mom held my hand as we walked in the front door of the dojo (karate school) one early Saturday morning. Strangely, I can recall wearing green corduroy pants and a shirt with green and brown strips running across it. Walking in the front door, I was greeted with what seemed like a massive cave with wooden floors, mirror-lined walls, and a rack filled with all sorts of interesting weapons at the other side of the room. My Sensei (teacher) said hello and taught me a few basic things like how to stand at the "yoi" (ready) position, how to "rei" (bow) and how to sit in "seiza" (sitting) position on the insteps of my feet. I can remember that all of it seemed fascinating to me
Transition 2	But the thing that would really leave an impression on me and set me off in a new direction (though I didn't know it at the time) came a few years later when I was ten years old and my mom dropped me and my friend Craig off at the dojo.
Event 2	As we walked in, we knew something was terribly wrong because the room was packed with adults wearing black belts that signified their high rank. Craig and I made our way through the crowd and were almost to the back of the room when the door opened again and a wave of silent electricity washed through the room. Suddenly, everyone in the dojo turned toward the door in unison
Event 3	It took me a while before I was able to peek around the adults and see who was at the center of all this attention. When I finally did manage to catch a glimpse, I observed an Okinawan man not much taller than myself wearing a crisp, white uniform and a worn-out black belt. He had a shaved head, a missing toe on his left foot, and large black pupils. There was no question to me then or now that he was by far the most intense and powerful presence that I'd ever experienced in my young life.

Breakdown of Narrative Components in "Sensei Chinen"	
Transition 3	The evening carried on and it was loud, hot, and crowded. He barked commands in a deep, penetrating voice that were half in English and half in Japanese. Even without seeing him, I could sense his silent presence as he floated by, causing my muscles to tense and my hair to stand on end. There seemed to be a physical aura that surrounded him, warning of his power and intensity.
Event 4 (Climax)	At one point, he lined everyone up in rows and told us all to lie down on our backs. We did this obediently and were further instructed to elevate our shoulders and legs off the ground and use our fists to pound on our bellies to condition the muscles. We all followed suit counting off painful blows in Japanese: ichi (one)... ni (two)... san (three)... shi (four)... go (five)... roku (six)... shichi (seven)... hachi (eight)... kyu (nine)... ju (ten).... But as this went on, he began to go down each of the rows using his fists to test the strength of our stomach muscles himself. I was at the end of a long line of adult black-belts and became increasingly nervous as he continued down the row testing one student after another. My friend Craig was so shaken by this that he got up and left the room. (I later learned they had to call his parents to come pick him up early because he was so upset.) I was no less scared, but responded by staying put and just closing my eyes as he worked his way closer and closer, the strained sounds of pain and exertion filling the crowded space. Finally, he arrived at the man next to me. For whatever reason, the conditioning went especially hard on him. I could hear the dull thud of fists on the man's stomach as he howled in pain, crying out "onegai shimasu, Sensei!, onegai shimasu, Sensei!" But when he finally got to me, he was much less violent and the trial was soon over. I was afraid, but for no reason.
Event 5	A few weeks later both Craig and I received a letter in the mail from Sensei Chinen. In the letter he said he hoped he hadn't frightened me too much, but that he could also remember being scared of his Sensei when he was a little boy. It was short, but it carried a powerful message and inspiration that follows me to this day: A good teacher should be compassionate, but also intense, perhaps even a bit fierce and frightening, because the most important lessons we learn are hard-won and require courage.
Value Statement (Moral)	So as a student I learned the value of courage, and as a teacher I learned the value of intensity. Thus, as you finish this course, I encourage you to go forward learning courageously and teaching intensely.

Explanation of Narrative Components

- Background 1: Explains why the story is being told.

- Background 2: This is a general background intended to transport the reader/listener into the world of the story

- Background 3: This is a personal background intended to get the reader/listener to identify with me as the person who is telling the story.

- Transition 1: This is labeled a transition because it carries the reader from background information into a specific event. As you will learn in Chapter Three, an event occurs in continuous space and time where something happens to someone.

- Event 1: The first event is meant to introduce and familiarize the reader/listener with the setting that the climax will eventually take place in.

- Transition 2: This transition is simply intended to indicate the passage of time.

- Event 2: The second event provides the first "lead-in" to the climax. Lead-ins set up the scene and build suspense.

- Event 3: Events two and three are separate from each other because of the phrase "It took me a while." Remember that an event occurs in continuous space/time. Because the storyteller says that time has passed, a new event has automatically begun.

- Transition 3: This transition is simply intended to indicate the passage of time.

- Event 4: The fourth event of the story is the climax or "common end" that all the other events have been leading up to. It represents the purpose the story was told and is the moment that the protagonist learns his lesson. The climax of the story always occurs when the opposing forces of the narrative confront each other directly. In this case, the opposing forces of the narrative were me and Sensei Chinen.

- Event 5: In literary theory, event five might be referred to as the dénoucment, wherein the final pieces of the narrative are explained or resolved. However, its main purpose is to set up the "value statement" or "moral" of the story.

- Value Statement.

MAUTHAUSEN

When I was seventeen years old, I was fortunate enough to travel on a three week European tour with the People to People Student Ambassador program. While it was fun being a tourist, seeing priceless art pieces in the Louvre, traveling by train throughout the Swiss Alps, and exploring an Austrian salt mine, the most significant, life altering experience came on the summer day that I entered the massive entrance gate to Mauthausen, an Austrian concentration camp.

That morning I rode the tour bus through small and large European towns. Roadways connected areas together—civilization surrounded us as buildings, farms, cars, and people blurred by. We rounded a bend, drove up a secluded hill, and were met with the sight of gray stone guard towers and barbed wire-covered walls. It felt like there was no turning back.

One of the first areas I was able to explore was the prisoners' living quarters. There were still holes in the wooden floor where men and women had to relieve themselves. I saw bare wooden bunks, narrow and hastily made, where up to five prisoners were forced to rest their heads after working over fourteen hours a day. I had read stories about such things, but being able to feel the splintered wood was a jolt of reality.

A defining element of Mauthausen was not the fact that it was a labor camp, where prisoners were forced to endure inhumane conditions for the sake of the Nazi regime—there were many such camps like that—but that the death rate here exceeded all other labor camps. This was mostly attributable to the granite quarry that occupied a large area of the camp. I slowly went down the 186 narrow, almost un-walkable, stone steps that led from the upper walkways into the actual quarry where inmates picked up granite slabs (weighing up to 110 pounds) and then had to make the return trip back up the aptly-named "Stairway of Death." This task, by itself, seemed insurmountable, but the tales shared of prisoners falling while climbing, creating a monstrous "domino effect," were truly terrifying.

Once I climbed out of the quarry area, and walked through a few rows of barracks, our group was led into a separated building and down a short flight of stairs. I stepped inside the next room, and tried to take everything in—the white walls, the signs labeling "Gaskammer," the metal piping along the walls. The room was bigger and lighter than I imagined it would be. Behind me, around me, people gathered, and we shuffled in toward the center of the room. My eyes traveled up, finding the ceiling, and it was then I saw the faucet heads. I felt the breath leave my lungs. My body started to shake, and I felt myself turn inward. Earlier, I was merely a bystander, a witness: I saw the bunks, I felt the stones in the quarry, I imagined standing for roll call in the courtyard—but in this place, with the walls closing in as more people entered, and the false hope of a shower pushing out the devastating fear of impending death, I felt an empathy stronger than I'd ever felt before. A guttural sob escaped from my lips as tears streamed down my face. I started to collapse, and found the ability to leave the room only when one fellow traveler held onto my right arm and another grabbed onto my left. We made our way out of the chamber and into the sunlight, relishing in the open air and sense of innate life.

I leaned against a barracks wall, trying to regain composure. I looked around as people passed by, continuing on with their tours and walking where I had just walked. A woman who worked as a guide stopped nearby to wait for her group to catch up. She caught my eye, assessed my stance, and sent me a brief nod; an acknowledgment, an understanding. Before I could stop myself, I heard myself ask, "How do you stand it? Being here, every day? Surrounded by death and torture and horror?" Without a moment to think, full of certainty and conviction, the tour guide responded in accented English, "I share these memories to people who do not know. Every day I remember who walked through these gates and died in these walls. I keep them alive. We all keep them alive. Their stories must be shared. We must remember."

My most extraordinary real-life lesson in the importance of communication occurred on a hot summer day in the Austrian hills, surrounded by the ghosts of the past. It is not enough to speak for the sake of talking, or to pretend to listen when others choose to tell us their stories. Every time we do this, we are wasting rare, precious opportunities for personal growth. But, when we choose to engage with one another as the tour guides do every day in Mauthausen; when we take the time to understand the message the other person is sending us, like when the stories were shared about the prisoner's hardships and the survivor's victories; it is in these everyday moments that we are forever changed.

Following the first example, provide a chronological breakdown of narrative components in "Mauthausen." In the left-hand column, identify the narrative component (background, event, or transition) and in the right-hand column, provide a brief description.

Breakdown of Narrative Components in "Mauthausen"	

Breakdown of Narrative Components in "Mauthausen"

Corresponding to your chronological breakdown of narrative components, explain the function of each narrative component in "Mauthausen" below:

HOWARD DEAN

It was ten years ago that I departed my grandmother's one bedroom apartment in Harrison, New Jersey, left my newly attained job at MTV in Manhattan, NY, and embarked on a journey of American Democracy in the heartland of Des Moines, Iowa. A once-in-a-lifetime opportunity arose after countless hours of netroots organizing through Meetup.com in New Jersey, to join a maverick presidential candidate as a paid full-time staffer. I had never been to the Midwest and didn't know what to expect but I was now working for the first netroots campaign in United States history for Governor and Doctor Howard Dean of Vermont.

I departed Newark Liberty International and arrived at Des Moines International Airport. An airport shuttle that would take me to campaign headquarters in the industrial part of town picked me up. I was slouched in my seat, head down, reading a text on my flip cell phone, and excited but nervous for this new chapter in my life. However, it so happened a New York Times journalist was sitting next to me, and quickly struck up a conversation. She started asking me all types of questions. "Where are you from? Which campaign are you working for? How did you get involved? Is this your first presidential campaign? Are you paid? Are you getting medical benefits?"

I then proceeded to adjust my posture in my seat, pick my head up, and look straight into the soul of this reporter and slowly and calmly answer each of her questions. "Hi, I am actually from Harrison, N.J., I left my job in the traffic department at MTV to join this presidential campaign because I am concerned about the direction of our country. I have never been involved in politics, and I, like many supporters, got involved in the campaign through our netroots organizing on Meetup.com. I was brought into the Dean campaign as a full-time paid staffer and we are the only presidential campaign offering staffers full medical benefits."

I recall this is the very moment I started to realize the importance of strategic communication, the consequences of improper interpersonal communication, and how, when you provide a story for others, it assists your audience in the retention and recall of critical information.

Narratives have always been a strong component of American presidential campaigns, and are even more important today due to our heavy reliance on mass media in modern political communication. The Dean campaign narrative focused on the success of an unknown candidate, who surged in the public opinion polls, and was fueled by individual supporters who mobilized online organizing and fundraising through the early Web 2.0 technologies of a campaign blog, and the use of Meetup.com for local monthly meetings.

The candidate's stump speeches focused on the rhetorical line, "You have the power to change this country, because the power is in your hands, not mine." This short sound bite fit well within our 24-hour legacy media landscape, played well in online videos, and also enabled individual supporters to feel they were an active part of the campaign. We as Americans are many times receptive to populist political narratives as this one, and the use of "you" and "yours" were the persuasive words that empowered individual supporters to volunteer, donate money, and change our country's destiny.

After many long workdays, late nights drinking Pepsi and eating pizza, the Iowa Caucus, a first in the nation vote was to take place on January 19, 2004. The tension was high in the Des Moines campaign headquarters. We were clearly leading the polls, but the other candidates were starting to close in on us, but we had confidence that Iowa was ours to win. The night of the caucus I was out in one of the volunteer camps of the "Perfect Storm," which was thousands of volunteers who were converging on Iowa to assist us in GOTV, or getting out the vote. The caucuses started that night and my colleague and I decided to drive back to campaign headquarters for the victory speech. Imagine now thousands of staffers, volunteers, and supporters packed into a hall in Des Moines, Iowa. The entire crowd was waving American flags as the candidate took the stage; a large American flag was the backdrop to the stage. Every national, international, and online media outlet was present. The noise in the room was at rock concert decibels, the stage was actually shaking from people stomping the floor, and the people-powered Howard Dean campaign had just come in a shocking third place in the Iowa caucus. Public speaking moments like these are always difficult, but the speaker has power, and can create a political narrative for the media, its citizens, and a nation that can last a generation.

The candidate began his speech thanking everyone, and then proceeded to react to the energy of the room. As the candidate started listing the states they would win in the upcoming primaries the crowd got louder and more boisterous. At a certain point the cheering of the crowd clearly drowned out much of the candidate's speech. The candidate was using a unidirectional microphone, which had a direct feed to the television media, and filtered out the crowd noise. The crowd in the hall assumed this speech was energy driven to inform the audience to continue on in the fight for the White House. We all thought it was a good speech to carry on in the political campaign to other states.

While we were driving back to the campaign headquarters, my brother-in law in New Jersey called and first thing he said was, "Have you turned on the television? Check out every network's coverage. What happened? Why did your candidate lose his mind?

As we entered the campaign headquarters it was eerily quiet; people were in obvious shock, as if it was all over. I saw the first coverage of the speech upstairs in the media office. Every network was playing a 28-second sound bite on repeat from the 35-minute speech. It was, "Not only are we going to New Hampshire, Tom Harkin, we're going to South Carolina and Oklahoma and Arizona and North Dakota and New Mexico, and we're going to California and Texas and New York … And we're going to South Dakota and Oregon and Washington and Michigan, and then we're going to Washington, D.C., to take back the White House! Yeah!!!" This was part of the media's interpretation and the narrative of our political campaign. The infamous Dean Scream as the media referred to it became an instant hit, and was one of the first examples of Web 2.0 memes online during American political campaigns. Hundreds of mashups were posted online as satire of the Dean Scream and our campaign was finished.

My bachelor of arts and master of arts in communication, and all the courses I had taken had prepared me for the power of public communication. However, it takes real life scenarios like these to test a human's unique ability to construct effective communication skills in different environmental contexts. Most important, I focused on providing a personal narrative for this reporter, who then could inform the citizens of a nation about an upstart presidential campaign. In the second scenario, the mass media chose to focus on a 28-second sound bite of the candidate's speech, which provided a story of our candidate and our campaign. As you will soon witness in this textbook, we are firmly focused on storytelling and the power of narrative because it is the essence of all successful public speaking.

Following the first example, provide a chronological breakdown of narrative components in "Howard Dean." In the left-hand column, identify the narrative component (background, event, or transition) and in the right-hand column, provide a brief description.

Breakdown of Narrative Components in "Howard Dean"	

Breakdown of Narrative Components in "Howard Dean"

Corresponding to your chronological breakdown of narrative components, explain the function of each narrative component in "Howard Dean" below:

Our Stories

Chapter One:
Backstage

Chapter One is titled "Backstage" because it provides you with a very basic foundation in communication models and outlines the differences between public speaking, which is the focus of this book, and conversation, which belongs to a more general study of human interpersonal communication.

Models of Communication

Aristotle

A communication model is a figure that attempts to symbolically represent a communicative process. One of the oldest communication models was described by Aristotle in his ancient text, The Rhetoric (ca. 330 BCE). Aristotle identified the communicative process as having four steps, originating with the speaker (i.e., the source) and terminating with the audience (i.e., the destination). Mediating between source and destination, however, are two additional steps: the argument and the speech itself.

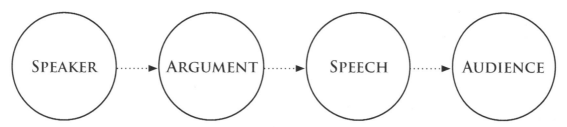

An argument refers to the abstract relationships among logic, reasoning, and evidence, but the form that the argument takes is the speech itself which refers to the specific way the argument is executed and includes all verbal, nonverbal, and organizational choices the speaker makes. In other words, the speech is the form and the argument is the content.

Lasswell

With the emergence of communication as an academic discipline in the twentieth century, theorists began to use models to understand communication as a more general process that occurred outside the circumscribed context of rhetoric and persuasion. Harold Lasswell (1960), for example, famously defined the process of communication as a question of "who says what to whom in what channel with what effect?" Observe that there are some similarities to Aristotle's model if we consider "who" to be the speaker, "whom" to be the audience, "what" to be the argument, and the "channel" to be the speech. Though, Lasswell's model implies applicability outside of the public speaking context because "who" and "whom" might represent many different relationships beyond speaker and audience.

Beyond providing a more generalized understanding of communication, Lasswell's model is also important because it considers the effect of the message on the audience. Another important feature of the Lasswell model is that it distinguishes between message (what) and medium (channel). Thus, when a communicator goes about designing an effective message, he or she should seriously take into account the medium through which the message will pass. For a speaker, this means accounting for the dynamics of the environment where the speech will be presented.

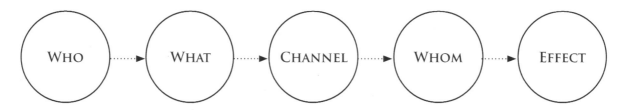

SHANNON/WEAVER

Claude Shannon and Warren Weaver provide a more detailed linear model of the communication process based on their work engineering telephone systems at Bell Labs. They offer nine steps, which include (1) information source, (2) sent message, (3) transmitter, (4) sent signal, (5) channel, (6) received signal, (7) receiver, (8) received message, and (9) destination. The key innovation of the Shannon/Weaver model is that messages are transmitted and received through the channel as signals. While this may appear only to apply to electronic communication, it highlights the importance of encoding and decoding in human language. Language is a set of agreed upon meanings that are associated with words and word combinations. To speak, one must encode thought into language, but to understand, one must decode language into thought.

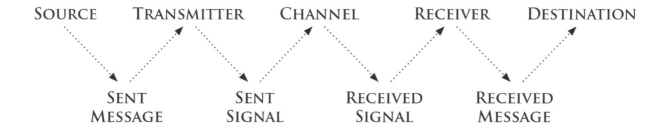

Another important contribution of the Shannon/Weaver model is the concept of noise. Noise is defined as anything that interferes with the transmission of the signal or message. Noise can come from an external source as when something interferes with signal transmission, or it can come from an internal source, as when prejudices or distracting thoughts prevent a receiver from clearly interpreting the message.

INTERACTION MODELS OF COMMUNICATION

Interaction models of communication, including Dance (1967), DeVito (2003), Schramm (1955), Thayer (1968), Wood (1997), and others attempt to account for communication as dynamic process which is inadequately characterized by models with discrete steps. In an attempt to capture more of the complexity of human interaction, theorists have used terms like "feedback" and "field of experience." Feedback refers to a receiver's response to a message as it is being received. Field of experience refers to the context used to generate or interpret a message. All communication relies to some extent on a shared field of experience. For example, you are able to read this text and I am able to write it because you and I share the English language within our field of experience.

WHY STUDY COMMUNICATION MODELS?

Communication models are helpful for improving public speaking because they help identify where problems occur and allow us a chance to diagnose and fix those problems. Linear models of communication (Aristotle, Lasswell, Shannon/Weaver) teach us that it can be useful to view speech preparation as a process moving from (1) topic selection to (2) research to (3) message construction to (3) practice to (4) performance. Conversely, the interaction models teach us to account for "field of experience" when crafting a message and to be sensitive to audience feedback when delivering a message.

You can also use models (later referred to as "mind mapping") to design the structure of your speech. The following exercise will familiarize you with the skills of model design.

Chapter One: Backstage

Exercise (Communication Models): Draw your own public speaking model below using the following bank of terms. Be sure to use each term only once.

Speaker	Argument	Speech	Audience	Effect	Field of Experience
Message	Channel	Encoding	Decoding	Noise	Feedback

DIFFERENCES BETWEEN PUBLIC SPEAKING AND CASUAL CONVERSATION

It might already be obvious to you from your own experiences that there are some substantial differences between public speaking proper and casual conversation. Let's outline some of these differences to better understand what's expected of us when we stand before an audience to deliver a speech.

- Whereas casual conversation is *impromptu*, public speaking is *prepared*.
  - »» Impromptu refers to a style of speaking that is spontaneous and lacking specific preparation. Public speaking tends to be extemporaneous, meaning that the speaker has prepared and practiced extensively, but addresses the audience directly and naturally.

- Whereas casual conversation is *reciprocal,* public speaking is *one-sided*.
  - »» Conversation, as the term implies, is reciprocal and depends on the give and take between two communicators. Public speaking tends to be one-sided and requires an audience to listen as the presenter shares his or her ideas, though it should be noted that the best public speakers build conversational cues into their speech to create a more natural and engaging relationship with the audience.

- Whereas casual conversation is *fluid and spontaneous*, public speaking is *focused*.
  - »» Unlike casual conversation, which tends to move fluidly from topic to topic depending upon the whims of the speakers, public speaking stays focused by remaining on a single topic and elaborating upon one central idea and its related main points (see Chapter Five).

- Whereas casual conversation is guided by *social norms*, public speaking follows a specific *protocol*.
  - »» Interpersonal communication research has demonstrated the existence of unconscious, informal rules we follow in conversation, such as taking turns, allowing others to speak, and cues to starting and ending conversations. In the public setting, however, the rules are formalized. Audiences do not peak during the performance, questions and comments are postponed, and audience members are expected to listen closely to the presentation.

- Whereas casual conversation usually involves only a *few* people, public speaking may involve *many*.
  - »» Though this may seem incidental to the content and delivery style of the speech, it is certainly not. Large audiences require a very different approach to delivery and may require additional technology (e.g., microphones, loudspeakers, jumbotron monitors).

Chapter Two: What's Your Story?

This chapter takes you through the process of figuring out what you want your speech to be about. Before starting work on your speech, you will need to consider a series of questions meant to determine your topic (the subject of your speech). These questions apply to the audience, the occasion, the environment, and, of course, your own personal interests, expertise, and ideas. You will also need to consider what you want to accomplish with your speech. That is, what is its purpose?

It Starts with You

Before you decide upon your general and specific purpose, before you even concern yourself with audience, context, and environment, you must take yourself into consideration. After all, you will be the one giving the speech and your success as a speaker will be based on your relationship to the topic you have chosen.

Remember the three stories at the beginning of the book? If you were to write a short story about something important that happened to you, what would it be? To be a good speaker you must find your "authentic self." Fortunately or unfortunately, there's no secret formula or instructions you can follow to do this. You must listen to your own voice and examine your experiences carefully. From this, you will hopefully determine what your motivation and passion is. Only you know what it is and if it's right for you. If you can identify something you're good at, that you enjoy and have a lot of experience with, and that other people would benefit from learning, then you're on the right track.

Exercise (Finding an Authentic Topic)

Use the table below to identify unique and important experiences you've had with your interests and talents. Once you've done this, start to consider how these experiences, interests, and talents might be applied to a particular subject or topic. The stronger the relationship that exists between these four items, the more likely you have found your authentic topic.

Experiences	Interests	Talents	Application

Experiences	Interests	Talents	Application

Audience Analysis

Once you've examined your own experiences, interests, talents, and the ways they can be applied, the next step is to think about your audience. In public speaking, it's not possible to think about each audience member as thoroughly as you think about yourself, so you need to consider more efficient ways of learning about them.

One way you can get to know your audience is by studying their **demographics.** Demographics are qualities specific to a group that include age, sex, gender, race, nationality, ethnicity, culture, sexual orientation, and other variables. Another, more obvious, way you can learn something about your audience is through *motivation*. Why are they there? Are you holding a seminar on how to start a small business? Perhaps you're giving a speech at a family reunion, or presenting research at an academic conference. In each of these cases, and the multitude of others that are possible, something about the audience is revealed just based on their presence in your audience.

Based on demographics and motivation, you might be able to make some guesses about the attitudes, beliefs, and values of your audience.

Attitudes: Disposition toward someone or something (i.e. liking or disliking).
Beliefs: Ideas about truth or falsehood.
Values: Deeply held personal judgments about right and wrong.

For example, a political party will likely share some core social and economic values, just as a particular religious group may share in common metaphysical, spiritual, and moral values. Various other interest groups (business owners, teachers, doctors, lawyers, parents, etc.) will also have a general set of attitudes, beliefs and values that they share in common. In some cases, it may be necessary to consult social scientific research (such as sociology and psychology journals) to better understand the common attitudes, beliefs, and values of a particular group.

Warning: Be careful not to overgeneralize. Just because a group tends to share certain ideas, doesn't mean that every member of that group feels exactly the same way. Making broad assumptions and general statements about a group (especially one that you are not a member of) can get you in a lot of trouble with the audience and seriously harm your credibility.

Communication Context and Environment

Context refers to the symbolic speaking environment (aka "occasion"), whereas **environment** is the physical space where the speech is given.

Contexts	Environments
Academic Conference	Lecture Hall
Business Meeting	Conference Room
Wedding	Church, Synagogue, Mosque
Job Interview	Office or Conference Room
Political Rally	Town Hall
Televised Speech	Television Studio

Whenever possible, you should take the opportunity to visit your speaking environment before you deliver your speech. Ideally, you would practice the speech a few times in the environment before it was time to perform. At minimum, you should be aware of the norms and expectations dictated by the context, and you should take control of the environment to meet the needs of your speech. For example, it would be inappropriate to provide personal testimony about your intuitions and personal beliefs at a scientific conference. In that setting, empirical evidence is the only thing that matters. Also, in terms of environment, don't be afraid to rearrange furniture or ask audience members to relocate before you begin speaking, as this demonstrates confidence and allows you to craft a more comfortable space to present.

YOUR GENERAL AND SPECIFIC PURPOSE

Taking into account the factors of audience, context, and environment discussed above, you should decide upon a general and specific purpose for your speech.

The **general purpose** refers to the overarching goal of the speech and may be to (1) inform, (2) persuade, or (3) entertain.

The purpose of an informative speech is to share information in the form of a **lesson.**

The purpose of a persuasive speech is to advocate for particular attitudes, beliefs, values, and/or actions in the form of a **proposition.**

The purpose of an entertainment speech is to engage and transport the audience through the use of narrative.

The **specific purpose** refers to the goal of the speech itself and is dependent upon the topic and central idea you have chosen. Ultimately, to determine your "specific purpose" you have to ask yourself what you want the audience to do with the information you give them. Should they come away with a different attitude about something? Should they change their beliefs or values? Should they behave differently?

Overall Questions to Consider when Selecting a Topic

- Your experiences, interests, and talents.

- Who is the audience? What are their demographics?

- What are the needs of the audience? (Do they need information? Do they want to be entertained? Should they be persuaded to do something that might help them in some way?)

- What are the audience's expectations? (What rules are dictated by the context?)

- Why should the audience care about this topic?

- What are my goals in speaking to this audience?

- Will the audience be receptive or skeptical? Friendly or hostile?

- Will the audience be voluntary? Are they being incentivized in some way?

- What questions might come from the audience at the conclusion of my speech?

In addition, the topic you choose should be:

- Timely and relevant to the audience

- Based on research instead of "common sense."

- Well-established with credible sources.

- Interesting and engaging to the audience.

- Commensurate with the audience's level of knowledge on the subject.

- Authentic: based on your own experiences, interests, and talents.

Exercise (Audience Analysis): You are working for an advertising firm that represents "solar roadways" (http://www.solarroadways.com/intro.shtml), a startup company whose mission it is to gather energy and provide power by gradually replacing roadway systems with solar panels that are designed to be driven on. Soon you'll be going on a speaking tour to towns and cities across the nation. What sort of audience questionnaire might you develop to prepare for your presentation? List five questions below.

Exercise (General and Specific Purpose): Go to the TED website (http://www.ted.com/) and select/view any three of the speeches listed below by typing the titles into the search box. Once you have completed viewing each speech, identify its general and specific purpose.

Speech	General Purpose	Specific Purpose
How Schools Kill Creativity		
The Puzzle of Motivation		
The Surprising Science of Happiness		
Your Elusive Creative Genius		
The Paradox of Choice		

Exercise (Topic Selection): A mind map is a method of organizing your ideas and narrowing down your topic by diagramming the relationship between your topic, central idea, main points, and pieces of evidence. This is an excellent way to brainstorm for an informative or persuasive speech. Use the space provided below (or a separate sheet) to map out your topic choices. For more information on "central idea" and "main points," skip ahead to Chapter Five.

Chapter Three: A Tale of Three Speeches

In the following chapter, you will be introduced to the definitions, components, and criteria for narrative, informative, and persuasive speaking.

Narrative Speech

Narrative is the oldest form of human cultural transmission. Historically, human beings have used narrative for many purposes, including teaching, entertainment, ritual performance, cultural production, and persuasion. Unlike informative and persuasive speech, however, narrative speech does not have a predefined purpose. A narrative speech might be used to entertain, but it might also be used to teach or persuade as well. Therefore, we should look to the principles of narrative speech as tools capable of achieving many functions, including persuasion and teaching.

What features define a narrative? Since we've determined that a narrative is not defined by its purpose, we should provide a definition based on its structure. For our purposes then, **a narrative is a series of events linked to one another to achieve a climax.** So, a narrative must have "a series of events," these events must be "linked," and they must achieve a "climax." Let's define these terms:

- An **event** is a continuous span of time and space that occurs in a **setting**, involving one or more characters, and featuring one or more **actions**. A setting refers to a physical place, a **character** refers to a person in a narrative, and an action refers to something that happens. The *central character* in a narrative is referred to as the **protagonist**, the character through whom we experience the story. Put most simply, an event is defined when someone does something somewhere, or when something happens to someone somewhere. Please note that a single event may contain multiple characters and actions, but never multiple settings or time spans.

- A narrative is defined above as a **series of events**. This means that a single event is not enough to form a narrative. Literary theorist Brian McFarlane (1996) refers to the timeline of events that comprise a narrative as "distributional functions" because events are distributed across the time and space of the story. McFarlane further divides distributional functions into "cardinal functions" (those events that are essential to the narrative) and "catalysers" (supportive actions). When organizing a narrative, it is essential to distinguish between essential and nonessential information. Cardinal functions are essential information.

- **Linkages** (or connections) bind events together into a single discernable narrative. Without clear linkages, events appear random and jumbled and the narrative is lost because it becomes impossible to follow. All narratives make use of **chronology** (ordering of events based on time) to form linkages, even if they don't adhere to a strictly chronological presentation of events. In selecting events to construct a narrative, the storyteller or narrator must consider the relationships between these events. For example: Which is the correct order of events? What prior knowledge does the audience need in order to correctly interpret the meaning of specific events? What is the cause/effect relationship between events? The best narratives are "tight" in the sense that they only include events that have a causal relationship to other events. **Digressive events** take the narrative off course and loosen the relationships between events.

- The **climax** is the raison d'être (French for "reason for existence") of the narrative and is the determining factor in deciding which events should be included in the narrative. **The climax is thus defined as the event wherein the opposing forces of the narrative finally meet and consequently resolve the underlying tension or suspense.**

- Though it is not mentioned in the basic definition of narrative provided above, **background information** often plays a critical part in a successful narrative. Names, dates, summaries, persistent conditions, etc., all count as background information. Background information is best understood in opposition to the events themselves. Whereas events take place at a particular time and location, background information is diffuse and general. As a test, one might ask when and where the information is situated. If there isn't a specific answer, it's probably background information.

NARRATIVE SPEECH STRUCTURE
Elements of a successful narrative speech include the following:

Transportation

The audience should feel transported by the speaker's combined use of vivid description and delivery performance. Vivid descriptions are defined below. Delivery is discussed in a separate section and refers to posture, gesture, eye contact, facial expressions, paralanguage, chronemics, and proxemics (see Chapter Six).

Background

Background information should provide enough information for the audience to grasp the context of the story being told. Names, dates, summaries of past events, and descriptions of persistent conditions might be included as background information.

Events

As indicated above, the story should contain multiple events each with a context, an agent (or agents), and an occurrence (or occurrences).

Transitions

Transitions are phrases that provide a segue between or among background information and events.

Organization

Good organization is dependent upon the establishment of an event-based chronology and development of clear causal linkages between events.

Climax

As indicated above, the climax is the event wherein the opposing forces of the narrative meet and resolve the underlying tension of the story. The underlying tension is created by an unfulfilled desire or need within the narrative's protagonist. This desire or need brings the protagonist into conflict with one of three forces: him/herself, someone else (another character), or some aspect of the physical world (e.g., nature). The climax is the basis upon which all other events are selected for the narrative.

Vividness

Vivid descriptions combine verbal and nonverbal dimensions. However, vivid descriptions can only be applied to events or emotional states. When describing events, special attention should be paid to settings, characters, and actions. The question of how to coordinate and organize descriptions can be difficult, but the best strategy is to describe the event one detail at a time through the eyes of the character and what he or she experiences. Along these same lines, emotional states like fear or anger can be conveyed by recourse to metaphor (e.g., "the rage burned within me like a fire"). On the delivery side, gestures, facial expressions, paralanguage, and proxemics can serve to vividly demonstrate events, rather than describe them. Delivery elements should be exploited wherever possible.

Re-entry

Just as the speaker transports the audience into the space of the story, he or she must also provide closure by indicating that the story is over and returning them home from the time and place of the narrative.

Chapter Three: A Tale of Three Speeches

Exercise (Basic Narrative Outlining): Create an outline of the following children's story by identifying (1) the series of events, (2) the linkages between them, (3) the climax event, and (4) any relevant background information. For reference, take a look at the story and outline in Appendix A: The Girl Without Hands

"The First Well" (http://www.bookbox.com/products/first-well?plang=eng-us)

(1) Series of events
- They was an out break of water
- The village came together to find a solution.
- The wise man who went north got a block of ice from the mountain and took it back to the village.
- There was a suggestion to place the water seed underground.
- The water seed devolved into the hole.

(2) The linkage between them. The farmers and the whole village stressed about not having water. They all worked together to get water to search.

3. Climax
- One of the generals brought back a small block of ice that he found at the mountain.
- The block of water was put into a whole where it disolve.
- The hole produced water for the village.

Exercise (Advanced Narrative Outlining): Go to the Moth website (themoth.org), select and listen to a speech of your choice, and create an outline of it by identifying (1) the series of events, (2) the linkages between them, (3) the climax event, and (4) any relevant background information. For an example of how to do this, go to Appendix B, Analysis of theMoth.org

INFORMATIVE SPEECH

Unlike the narrative speech, informative and persuasive speeches are defined by their purpose, and the purpose of an informative speech is to teach. **Teaching is the task of building knowledge in others**, so the whole purpose of this section is to teach how informative speeches effectively build knowledge in audiences.

To illustrate a critical point about the relationship between the narrative and informative speech, consider the fact that they are not mutually exclusive. Actually, narrative is the oldest method of teaching. Imagine, for example, how our distant ancestors must have gathered around tribal fires and shared stories of hunting, gathering, and discovery. Perhaps this ritual began as a form entertainment, but it was also adaptive in the sense that it spread information to the tribe and helped everyone to avoid danger and find shelter and nourishment. Consider also how the lessons of early religions and philosophies take the form of parables, allegories, and short stories. As our cultures became more complex, though, so did systems of building, storing, and sharing knowledge. The scientific revolution, specifically, had a key role in divorcing knowledge from narrative and presenting ideas out of their original contexts as testable hypotheses. As a result of this, teaching and presenting information took on a new form. To understand it, let's take a brief look at how the scientific method is articulated through the classical template of a research paper.

RESEARCH PAPER STRUCTURE

Introduction

This section is intended to introduce the topic and justify the need for investigation. The introduction may also identify the variables in question and end with a formal statement of the research question.

Example: The video game industry is tremendously large and many people spend a significant amount of time playing videogames.

Research Question

A research question is a statement of inquiry about the relationship between variables.

Example: What is the effect of videogames on cognition?

Literature Review

The literature review provides a history of previous scientific inquiry into the question under investigation.

Example: What prior research exists concerning videogames and cognition?

Hypothesis

The literature review should conclude with the statement of a hypothesis that asserts a relationship between variables.

Example: Depending on the research presented in the literature review, one might hypothesize a positive relationship: "videogames enhance cognition," a negative relationship: "videogames diminish cognition," or a null relationship: "videogames have no effect on cognition."

Method

The method describes how the hypothesis was tested. In quantitative social science research, there are three general ways to test a hypothesis: survey, experiment, and content analysis. Qualitative methods include ethnography, interviews, and text analysis (including discourse and rhetorical analysis). The example we're using is best tested using quantitative methods.

Example: An experiment is employed. A sample of individuals who do not regularly play videogames participate in this experiment. They are given a cognitive test to complete before being divided into two groups. The first group (the experimental group) is subjected to a regimen of playing videogames, but the second group (the control group) is given a regimen of neutral tasks to perform. When the regimens are completed, the groups are given a second cognitive test to complete. The data on the cognitive tests will then be analyzed within and between groups.

Procedure

The procedure describes how the method was applied. Step-by-step instructions for how to perform the experiments are provided in this section.

Example: (1) Volunteer participants arrived at the laboratory. (2) Participants were brought into a classroom, informed of their rights under the law, and provided with statements of informed consent that they were asked to sign. (3) Participants were administered a cognitive test with a time limit of thirty minutes. (4) Participants were randomly assigned to separate groups and led into individual cubicles. (5) The experimental group was assigned a regimen of videogames and the control group was a assigned a neutral task. (6) At the completion of the regimen, participants were brought back into the classroom and administered a second cognitive test.

Results

The results present an analysis of the data after it is gathered .
Example: Perhaps a statistical analysis of cognitive test scores between and within groups suggests that there's a significant mean difference in test scores for the experimental group, but not for the control group.

Discussion

The discussion is meant to interpret the results.
Example: Perhaps it was demonstrated that those in the experimental group had a significant improvement in cognitive test results in comparison to the control group.

Conclusion

The conclusion highlights the key findings of the research.
Example: If our example results were true, we might say that videogames enhance cognition.

INFORMATIVE SPEECH STRUCTURE

The conventional structure of an informative speech, while not identical to the format above, has many of the same characteristics, including an organization that is based on sections rather than on events. In general, the sections of the informative speech include:

Attention

The very first statement of the speech is intended to gain the audience's attention. This statement should be clearly related to the central idea and it shouldn't overwhelm the forthcoming message of the speech. Often, attention statements take the form of intriguing questions, surprising facts or observations, shocking measurements, or powerful quotations.

Central Idea

The statement which explains what the **lesson** of the informative speech is going to be about.

Importance

The statement of importance explains why the knowledge to be gained through the speech is important to the speaker and should be important to the audience.

Credibility

The statement of credibility is intended to demonstrate the competence of the speaker and win the trust of the audience.

Preview of Main Points

The preview of main points is a list of points that will be elaborated upon in the body of the speech. This preview is only intended as a "table of contents" or "roadmap" for the rest of the speech, it is not the place to elaborate on the points themselves.

In an informative speech, main points can be organized according to the strategies presented in the section titled "Strategies for Organizing Your Speech," which includes chronological, spatial, and topical. However, the principle of **complexity** should be considered when organizing a speech based on topic. This means that the simplest or most basic pieces of information should come before the more complex and advanced information.

Transition

The first transition combines verbal and nonverbal cues that the speaker is moving into the body of the speech.

Elaboration of Main Points

The main points are an extension of the central idea. Their purpose in the context of the informative speech is to explain, describe, and/or define the **lesson** as fully as possible. The main points must be supported by logic, reasoning, evidence, and research wherever possible.

Transition

The second transition combines verbal and nonverbal cues that the speaker is moving into the conclusion of the speech.

Recap of Main Points

Similar to the preview described above, the recap of main points is a list of points that have been elaborated upon in the body of the speech. Just as in the preview, the recap is not intended to elaborate upon the points or introduce new information.

Restatement of the Central Idea

The statement intended to remind the audience of the lesson.

Conclusive Statement

The conclusive statement is the very last statement of the speech and should be both concise and memorable.

It is clear from this comparison of scientific articles to informative speeches that the way we present knowledge has been transformed by science. Whereas in the distant past, knowledge was contextualized by direct, situated experience presented in narrative form, today it is presented more abstractly with the purpose of being applied to various situations. Instead of event-driven, chronological narratives, information is more often presented in the three-part structure of "introduction-body-conclusion," which is further subdivided into a series of sections united by a central idea, but discussed as discrete main points.

But this doesn't mean narrative has no role to play in informative speaking. To begin with, consider that the introduction-body-conclusion structure corresponds to the three-act structure of classical drama in which the audience is introduced to characters, presented with a conflict that leads to rising action, and finally confronted with a climax that restores order to the world of the story. Other ways that narrative tools still reverberate through informative and persuasive speaking include:

- **Brief Illustrations**: Short stories or anecdotes used to illustrate a point.

- **Extended Illustrations:** A full narrative (see the narrative speech section above) is used to illustrate the central idea of the speech.

- **Bracketing**: The same story is used at the beginning and end of a speech or repeatedly referred to throughout the speech to provide closure or evidence of the central idea.

In addition, when listening to a speech or using stories in your own speech, always consider the function of the story by asking yourself, "what does the story do?" Does the story serve to build credibility with the audience? Does it illustrate a main point or serve as evidence? Is the story intended to gain the audience's attention or provide a transition between sections or main points? In essence: "Why is the story being told?"

Furthermore, scientific articles and informative speeches do tell a certain kind of story and thus constitute a particular type of narrative. Specifically consider the *literature review* and *procedure* sections of a scientific article and how they "tell the story" of previous and current research. The best informative speeches also tell a story: the story of the speaker's journey of discovery through research, scientific investigation, and/or personal experience. This approach builds credibility and aids in comprehension because it takes the audience through the learning process that the speaker had to go through. Thus, good speakers are a lot like "information tour guides" who walk the audience through understanding one step at a time.

Exercise (Informative Outlining): You Create an outline of the following informative speech by identifying (1) Attention Statement, (2) Central Idea, (3) Importance, (4) Credibility, (5) Preview of Main Points, (6) Elaboration of Main Points, (7) Recap of Main Points, (8) Restatement of the Central Idea, and (9) Conclusive Statement. For reference, take a look at the informative speeches and outlines in Appendix C, Informative TED Talks. Also, identify all narrative features of the speech and explain their function (what informative role do they play?).
"How Economic Inequality Harms Societies" (Richard Wilkinson)
http://www.ted.com/talks/richard_wilkinson

Chapter Three: A Tale of Three Speeches

Chapter Three: A Tale of Three Speeches

PERSUASIVE SPEECH

In addition to presenting perhaps the oldest model of communication, Aristotle was also the first to closely analyze the art of persuasion ("**rhetoric**") by dividing it into three qualities: **ethos, pathos,** and **logos**. Ancient as these principles may be, they still describe the three major variables that contribute to or detract from the effectiveness of a persuasive appeal.

Ethos refers to spirit or character. A large part of the persuasive effectiveness of a message comes from the person who is presenting it. To test this idea, think about how you would respond to surprising information shared by a close friend whom you trust versus someone with a hidden agenda who had lied to you in the past. The very same words would likely be treated seriously in the first case and with great skepticism in the second. We know, therefore, that the reputation of the communicator plays an important role in the persuasive effectiveness of the message.

Credibility refers to the trust an audience places in the speaker, and it plays an important role in developing the sort of character audiences find persuasive. In practice, credibility is an evolving mixture of reputation and performance: what you've done in the past and what you're doing now. Every performance is simultaneously a risk and opportunity to one's reputation. Some theorists therefore divide credibility into three categories: **initial** (reputation), **derived** (earned during the performance), and **terminal** (the final impression of the speaker).

So what makes you trust a speaker? There are six primary qualities that enhance credibility: sameness, reputation, personal stakes, empathy, knowledge, intelligence, and personal experience.

- **Sameness:** For evolutionary reasons, people tend to place more credibility in those who are similar to themselves. Though unfortunate, this makes sense if you consider that most people tend to place a high degree of trust in themselves.

- **Reputation:** As referenced above, reputation is a critical factor in establishing credibility, but it's not just about past performance. Collective evaluation also plays an important role in shaping reputation. In other words, it's not just your performance, but how people collectively interpret and evaluate your performance that counts.

- **Personal Stakes:** What do you have to gain or lose with the success or failure of your persuasive appeal? The more clearly and obviously your personal stakes overlap with the collective stakes of your audience, the better your credibility will be.

- **Empathy:** The ability to relate emotionally to your audience is important to establishing credibility. Do you care about the things they care about? If you do, your credibility will increase.

- **Knowledge:** Your awareness of the facts related to your persuasive appeal increases credibility. If it becomes apparent that you lack important knowledge of information associated with your topic, audiences will have reason to doubt you. This is why it's important to choose a topic that you are interested in and willing to study carefully.

- **Intelligence:** Intelligence refers to the ability to manipulate knowledge to achieve specific outcomes. Without intelligence, knowledge is useless and without knowledge, intelligence is impotent. The audience will judge your intelligence on many factors, but foremost among them are the way you use language, your use of logic and reasoning, and your conclusions.

- **Personal Experience:** As discussed under the section on informative speech, science has revolutionized how we know the world by employing tools like sampling and inferential statistics to overcome the natural limitations of personal knowledge. However, we still place great importance on individual personal experience, and for good reason. Personal experience is the intimate testing ground for all theory. If something lacks the resonance of truth in our own experience (or in someone else's) we're less likely to buy into the persuasive message.

Pathos refers to the use or manipulation of emotions in persuasion. Even when logic, reasoning, evidence, and research are lacking, audiences may be moved by a speaker's passion. A **demagogue**, for example, is a speaker who makes use of emotion, prejudice, and fear to persuade an audience. To some extent, pathos is also dependent upon ethos. For an audience to be persuaded through a speaker's emotional manipulation, they must on some level trust in the character of that speaker.

How are emotions manipulated through speech? Topic choice, verbal cues, nonverbal cues, and presentation aids can all play a role in the manipulation of emotion in a speech.

- **Topic Choice:** Some topics lend themselves particularly well to emotional manipulation, while others do not. For example, the time-worn debate over abortion is so predisposed to emotional appeals that even when speakers attempt to approach it objectively the results are often clouded by pathos. Other topics like recycling are relatively less controversial on the surface, but can lend themselves to the use of emotion in the right context. Generally speaking, when you approach your topic from the perspective of **values** (deeply held personal judgments about right and wrong), pathos has a much greater chance of coming into play. **Attitudes** (liking or disliking) and **beliefs** (truth or falsehood) tend to be less volatile when challenged, though can still provoke strong emotions to the extent that they support value systems.

- **Verbal Cues:** Because we have a visceral reaction to some words based on their repeated use in previous contexts, it's possible to touch on an audience's emotions simply through words. Consider the differences between words like "ecstatic" vs. "glad" to describe happiness, "dejected" vs. "glum" to describe sadness, "terrified" vs. "anxious" to describe fear, and "tortured" vs. "hurt" to describe pain. In each of these pairs, the first word has more emotional impact than the second. However, sometimes language is used in an attempt to reduce the emotional impact of ideas. Former President George W. Bush and officials in his administration infamously substituted the words "enhanced interrogation" for "torture" to lessen the emotional response to policies on the handling of those held on suspicion of terrorism. When words are substituted in this way without significantly changing the meaning of what those words refer to, it's called **doublespeak**: language which is used to disguise meaning.

- **Nonverbal Cues:** Delivery is a holistic concept and therefore all aspects of nonverbal communication play a role in emotional persuasion, but there are still several key aspects that stand out: facial expressions, eye contact, and paralanguage.

  - »» **Facial Expressions:** Beneath the skin of our face, a layer of delicate interconnected muscles conveys happiness, sadness, pain, anxiety, anger, surprise, and a host of other more subtle emotions. Even when we don't want to show our emotions, they often betray us through facial expressions. In psychology, "emotional contagion theory" even suggests that looking at a face with a particular emotion on display transmits that emotion to the viewer. In other words, looking at happy faces makes us happy and looking at sad faces makes us sad.

  - »» **Eye Contact:** Looking at audiences directly and (in most cases) providing sustained, individualized eye contact is vital to emotional persuasion. As noted above, pathos is somewhat dependent upon ethos, and we tend not to trust other people and their emotional appeals when they don't look us in the eyes.

»» **Paralanguage:** In addition to being your primary means of communication in public speech, the voice is also a very sensitive conductor of emotion. Every subtlety of our present emotional state is broadcast through the voice. Absence of emotion in the voice is referred to as being monotone and that is to be avoided. The emotional tone of your voice should mirror the content of your speech and remain consistent throughout. For example, tragedy should be treated with a somber tone.

Logos refers to the use of logic to persuade an audience. Logic, reasoning, and evidence are the subjects of a separate section; however, it's vital to point out that logic does not reduce to simple "common sense." Common sense, though usually defined as "good judgment," is actually nothing more than a mixture of hearsay (unsubstantiated information) and popular opinion, and is used primarily for reasons related to political ideology. For example, "It's common sense that we need to lower taxes right now!" On the other hand, logic is a formal system of reasoning based on the internally consistent application of rules. The most fundamental distinction in logic exists between inductive and deductive logic.

- **Inductive Logic:** When we come to a general rule of understanding based on a collection of specific instances, we are using inductive logic. A classic illustration of inductive logic is the conclusion that all swans are white. This conclusion would likely be arrived at by someone who has only seen white swans and never seen a black swan. Of course, black swans do exist, so this example also reveals that inductive logic is imperfect when it does not account for every manifestation related to the conclusion.

- **Deductive Logic:** When we apply general rules (called premises) to specific instances, we are using deductive logic. The principles of deductive logic are summed up in the structure of the syllogism (a logical statement where a conclusion is drawn based on two premises that share a common term). Aristotle expresses a classic syllogism in the following figure:

> - **Premise 1:** Socrates is a man.
> - **Premise 2:** All men are mortal.
> - **Conclusion:** Socrates is mortal.

Persuasive Speech Structure

You will notice that the structure of the persuasive speech is the same as the informative. This is not by accident since a good persuasive speech should also have informative and narrative elements. Note, however, that the content and organization of a persuasive speech is quite different.

Attention

The very first statement of the speech is intended to gain the audience's attention. This statement should be clearly related to the central idea and it shouldn't overwhelm the forthcoming message of the speech. Often, attention statements take the form of intriguing questions, surprising facts or observations, shocking measurements, or powerful quotations.

Central Idea

In a persuasive speech, the central ideal is the **proposition** (statement that the speaker intends for the audience to accept). This may be a proposition of action, fact, policy, or value.

Importance

The statement of importance explains why it is important to the speaker that the audience accepts the proposition offered and why accepting the proposition should be important to the audience.

Credibility

The statement of credibility is intended to demonstrate the competence of the speaker and win the trust of the audience.

Preview of Main Points

The preview of main points is a list of points that will be elaborated upon in the body of the speech. This preview is only intended as a "table of contents" or "roadmap" for the rest of the speech, it is not the place to elaborate on the points themselves.

In a persuasive speech, evidence should dictate the order of presentation for the main points. As noted in the section titled "Strategies for Organizing Your Speech," chronological, spatial, topical, and problem/solution strategies might be employed. However, in addition to accounting for hierarchy of knowledge (as in the informative speech), the persuasive speech should also order the main points according to strength, since not all points are based on equally convincing evidence. In general, the principle of **recency** should be employed, wherein the strongest or most convincing points are saved for last. Alternatively, **primacy** may be used with skeptical or otherwise unreceptive audiences. Primacy places the most compelling evidence up front in an attempt to capture the interest and imagination of resistant listeners and get them to at least entertain the proposition. **Monroe's Motivated Sequence** is another, more specialized strategy, which employs visualization as a persuasive technique. Chapter Five provides some further details on Monroe's Motivated Sequence.

Transition

The first transition combines verbal and nonverbal cues that the speaker is moving into the body of the speech.

Elaboration of Main Points

The main points are an extension of the proposition. Their purpose in the context of the persuasive speech is to provide evidence and an argument that supports the proposition as fully as possible. The main points must be supported by research (see Chapter Four), evidence (the information gained from research), and logical reasoning (the use of evidence in forming a conclusion).

Transition

The second transition combines verbal and nonverbal cues that the speaker is moving into the conclusion of the speech.

Recap of Main Points

Similar to the preview described above, the recap of main points is a list of the arguments that have been elaborated upon in the body of the speech. Just as in the preview, the recap is not intended to elaborate upon the argument or introduce new evidence.

Restatement of the Central Idea

This statement is a restatement of the proposition.

Conclusive Statement

The conclusive statement is the very last statement of the speech and should be both concise and memorable. If appropriate, the conclusive statement should contain a "call to action" where the speaker urges the audience to act upon the proposition.

Exercise (Persuasive Outlining): Create an outline of the following persuasive speech by identifying (1) Attention Statement, (2) Central Idea, (3) Importance, (4) Credibility, (5) Preview of Main Points, (6) Elaboration of Main Points, (7) Recap of Main Points, (8) Restatement of the Central Idea, and (9) Conclusive Statement. For reference, take a look at the persuasive speeches and outlines in Appendix C, Persuasive TED Talks. Also, identify all narrative features of the speech and explain their function (what persuasive role do they play?).
"We the People and the Republic we must Reclaim" (Lawrence Lessig)
http://www.ted.com/talks/lawrence_lessig_we_the_people_and_the_republic_we_must_reclaim

Chapter Three: A Tale of Three Speeches

Exercise (Persuading with Ethos and Pathos): Using the speech video and your outline from the previous Exercise as a tool for analysis, answer the following questions: (1) How is credibility (ethos) established through all of the following tools that may apply: sameness, reputation, personal stakes, empathy, knowledge, intelligence, and personal experience. (2) How is emotion (pathos) manipulated through all of the following tools that may apply: topic choice, verbal cues (language), and nonverbal cues (facial expressions, eye contact, and paralanguage)?

Chapter Four: Getting Your Story Straight

Now that you understand the differences between narrative, informative, and persuasive speeches, and can identify the components of each, it's time to explore how to build your own speech presentations. Strictly narrative speeches were covered in the last chapter, though the principles of narrative will continue to shape our understanding of how to prepare and deliver informative and persuasive speeches.

In this chapter, you will learn to use research to explore your topic, gather evidence, and construct lessons and arguments based on principles of logical and ethical reasoning.

First, let's consider the purpose of performing research. Successful speakers use research to learn about their topic, not to find evidence for something they already believe is true. If you use research to support pre-existing conclusions, you're putting the cart before the horse and ultimately run the risk of diminishing your credibility by neglecting or misinterpreting key pieces of evidence. This can be very awkward if it's brought to your attention after your speech. But situations like this can be avoided by keeping an open mind and using research to learn rather than support "gut feelings" or conclusions you've already jumped to.

Use the following information on research and citations when investigating your topic:

With the single exception of the **impromptu** speech, all speeches require research. In some cases (like a personal narrative), the research takes the form of introspection and requires you to write down, review, and edit a series of events that you experienced. In most cases, however, such as informative and persuasive speeches, external sources are required for the overall success of the presentation.

Sources

Search engines (like Google, Ask, Yahoo, etc.) and user-edited resources (such as wikis) are not valid sources. A Google Scholar (scholar.google.com) search might point you in the right direction, but is not itself a source because Google Scholar doesn't author anything. It merely generates options based on algorithms. Below are several tiers of sources based on their reliability. You should always strive to use information from the top three tiers. *The best way to ensure you are selecting from a reliable source is to do your research using a library database and/or Google Scholar.*

1. Tier One

    a. Peer-reviewed journal articles and conference proceedings. These are research reports in science and the humanities that are reviewed by a select group of experts (published scholars) and are either rejected or accepted with revisions based on peer review.

    b. United States and international reports and agencies. The federal government gathers and publishes information through various agencies, bureaus, and departments such as the Securities and Exchange Commission (SEC), the Federal Communications Commission (FCC), the Food and Drug Administration (FDA), the Environmental Protection Agency (EPA), the Census Bureau, and many others (see USA.gov for a complete list). International agencies such as the United Nations (UN), the World Bank, and others publish similar reports. These reports gather information transparently and should not be confused with the "propaganda" generated by the rise of new political action committees or "PACs."

2. Tier Two

    a. Edited academic books. These are books that are composed of chapters written by different authors, but reviewed by one or more editors for content, quality, and accuracy. These books are usually published by university presses or other academic publishers (e.g., Sage, Oxford, Wiley-Blackwell, etc.).

    b. Academic books. These are books that are written by one or more authors with a college or university affiliation or by independent scholars. Like edited academic books, these are also usually published by university presses.

3. Tier Three

    a. Textbooks. These are books (like the one you're holding right now) that are meant for classroom instructional use and don't generally contain original research.

    b. Trade books. These books are published by (non-academic) commercial publishers and intended for a general readership.

d. Conference papers and posters. These are research reports in science and the humanities that are presented at professional conferences (some TED talks are exemplary of academic conferences, but there are a vast multitude of others in every discipline).

e. Publications offered by professional associations. If you visit the website of a professional academic association (e.g., National Communication Association, American Psychological Association), you will likely find general information on the field of study, important definitions, value statements, and the history of the organization. Many professional organizations publish journals. If these journals are peer reviewed (i.e., if they have a board of reviewers), these journals should be considered "tier 1" sources of information.

4. Tier Four

a. Other sources, such as documentary films, news reports, radio broadcasts, magazines, brochures and pamphlets, blogs, and personal interviews may (in some cases) be acceptable sources depending on how they are employed; however, they should be regarded with skepticism and further scrutinized for inaccuracy and bias. In general, reports offered by the *New York Times, National Public Radio*, the *British Broadcasting Corporation* and the *Public Broadcasting Service* tend to be more credible than most other sources.

TIPS AND TECHNIQUES FOR CITING SOURCES

You should strive to include a variety of evidence in each of your main points. This keeps the content interesting for the audience, and offers them the best chance to truly comprehend the topic. One way to remember this is to follow the S.A.F.E.S.T. approach to evidence:

- S - Statistic
- A - Analogy
- F - Fact
- E - Example
- S - Story
- T - Testimony

You don't need to include every form of evidence, but you should include enough to make your point in a variety of ways. The order is up to you, but should employ some organizational strategy and follow a hierarchy.

CITING SOURCES IN THE OUTLINE (APA IN-TEXT CITATIONS)

There are rules for citing sources according to APA standards, but this brief overview will cover the highlights. Most course instructors will expect you to cite a source every time you borrow information from it, whether you are quoting an author directly or paraphrasing in your own words. It is imperative that you double-check spellings of author/organization names, as well as years, to make sure that your in-text citations match the sources listed on the reference page.

- Direct Quote Citation Variations

  » One author/organization, one page: (Last name, Year, p. #)

    »» Ex. (Altieri, 2013, p. 4)

  » One author/organization, multiple pages: (Last name, Year, pp. #-#)

    »» Ex. (American Heart Association, 2012, pp. 6-7)

  » Multiple authors, one page: (Last name & Last name, Year, p. #)

    »» (Pallant & Jones, 2011, p. 18)

  » Multiple authors, multiple pages: (Last name & Last name, Year, pp. #-#)

    »» (Jones, Altieri & Pallant, 2014, pp. 29-30)

- Paraphrasing Citation Variations

  » One author/organization: (Last name, Year)

    »» (Pallant, 2013)

  » Multiple authors (Last name & Last name, Year)

    »» (Jones & Altieri, 2012)

- Citing Sources During Your Speech (Oral Citations)

    » It is important that you cite your sources in the outline, so that you and the course instructor are clear about where you obtained your information, but this does nothing to prove to your audience that you conducted adequate research for writing your speech. Therefore, you should orally cite your sources throughout the presentation as well.

» The first time you cite a source, you need to state these parts (in any order, before the research):

- Author Last Name(s) or Organization Name

- Year of publication, update, or copyright

- Title of the source

- Credibility of source (personal interview only)

» You also need to make it flow in the speech so that it sounds like a natural progression of thought. Words/phrases you might find useful to help with the flow of your speech include:

Informed	Wrote	Found	Stated
I read	According to	Posted on	Said
Reported	Explained	Thinks	Sought to discover
Believed	Described	Noted	Revealed
Demonstrated	Concluded	Featured	Analyzed

» Correct oral citations will sound something like this:

- According to Pallant's 2012 book "Tips and Tricks for Public Speakers"...

- In his 2013 article "The Meaning of Presentation Aids," Jones sought to discover...

- In "Reducing Communication Apprehension," written in 2011, Altieri informed the reader that...

- Once a source is fully cited, you can shortcut later oral citations in the speech by stating the

    Author Last Name(s) or Organization Name

    Title of the source

    Phrase "The same source..."

Logic, Reasoning, Evidence, and Ethics

Once you've gathered enough credible information about your topic, you can begin to form your central idea. Remember that informative speeches have **lessons** as their central ideas and persuasive speeches have **propositions**.

The next step is to identify your evidence and subject it to the rules of logical reasoning. For many informative speeches, you need only edit and organize your evidence according to a particular organizational strategy (see Chapter Five) such as **spatial**, **chronological**, and **topical** and make sure it progresses according to the **rule of complexity** (information should be presented in order from least complex to most complex). For some informative speeches, and all persuasive speeches, however, an additional set of steps is required to ensure the validity of the argument behind the proposition.

In the following section you will be introduced to **inductive, deductive,** and **causal** logic. Though you need not specifically mention any of these terms in your speech, you should be able to identify what kind of logic you're using in the interpretation of your evidence and in arriving at your conclusion (i.e., the central idea or "proposition" of your speech).

You will also learn about various other logical principles, tests for proving arguments, and methods of symbolically describing your argument. Don't be intimidated by the structure of the examples that follow. Not every example applies to every argument or proposition. These are only intended as tools for you to use in subjecting your evidence and conclusion to a rigorous logical test. However, also keep in mind that your ability to logically demonstrate the connection between your evidence and your conclusion will determine the success or failure of your argument and your persuasive speech.

As you progress through the following sections, consider at each turn how you might apply these principles to your own arguments.

Logic was previously defined (in opposition to common sense) as "a formal system of reasoning based on internally consistent application of rules." As such, it does not require empirical evidence to be validated, rather the opposite is true: when we gather empirical evidence, we subject it to the rigors of interpretation according to logical rules. For example, one very basic logical rule is **the rule of non-contradiction of terms**, meaning that something cannot exist in two mutually exclusive categories at the same time. For example, something cannot be both present and absent simultaneously.

There are many categories of logic, but two of the most fundamental are induction and **deduction.** Once again, induction occurs when we come to a general rule based on a collection of specific instances, and deduction occurs when we apply a general rule to a specific instance. The following are additional examples of **induction** and deduction:

Induction: Imagine you were born and raised in a small village where everyone spoke the same language and had no contact with the outside world. Using inductive logic in this circumstance you might come to the conclusion that your language is the only language in existence. And since this is an imaginary world we're talking about, you might be right (maybe there are no other languages and no other people). However, you might also be wrong because your range of experience isn't wide enough to capture the true scope of the world. It could be that outside your village there are cities where a multitude of different languages are spoken. When inductive reasoning goes wrong in this way, it is referred to as the **fallacy of overgeneralization**. When we make statements about things that exist beyond our experience, we are susceptible to this error in logic.

On the other hand, if you were to conclude that your language is the only one spoken in your village, you would be correct provided that you knew everyone in the village and could confirm they only spoke your language. Induction works out in this case because you have taken into consideration the entire universe of possible outcomes. Scientific researchers attempt to approximate this through **random sampling** (a technique for assessing or measuring an entire population based on a subset of randomly chosen subjects). As long as the entire population is accounted for and every subject has an equally likely chance of being selected, the sample has a high probability of representing the total population. It is thus critically important to know the parameters (limits or extent) of the population you are drawing conclusions about.

Exercise (Inductive Logic): Which of the following conclusions were arrived at through inductive logic (there may be more than one). Also, identify which conclusions are based on faulty logic and think about why the conclusions are faulty.

1. After I got into an accident with my car, I noticed that the tire pressure light stays on all the time. The accident must have damaged the tire pressure sensor.

2. We know that poverty and crime are problems in the inner city. We also know that there's more air pollution in the inner city. Air pollution may cause poverty and crime.

3. I exist and am conscious of my existence; therefore, my existence must have some broader universal significance beyond myself.

4. In the 1950s elevated incidence of lung cancer and other diseases was observed among people who smoke. Early studies on this led researchers to the conclusion that there may be a relationship between smoking and certain diseases such as lung cancer.

5. Humans have constructed buildings, cities, and even space stations. Therefore, someone or something must have built the earth and the universe.

6. On my geometry test, one of the problems was to determine whether or not a particular triangle was a "right triangle." None of the angle measurements were given, but two side measurements were given. I was able to solve the problem because I know the Pythagorean Theorem. What kind of logic did I use?

7. We haven't noticed any problems with climate change in my town; therefore, climate change is probably not a big problem.

8. My grandparents didn't go to college and neither did my parents, but they were able to make a good living. I don't think I need to go to college either.

9. Government is wasteful; therefore, we shouldn't have to pay any taxes.

Deduction: The syllogism is the quintessential example of deductive logic. Remember that a syllogism is a logical statement where a conclusion is drawn based on two premises that share a common term. Consider the following set of syllogisms carefully:

• **Premise 1:** All animals are mortal. • **Premise 2:** All humans are animals. • **Conclusion:** All humans are mortal.	• **Premise 1:** No reptiles have fur. • **Premise 2:** All snakes are reptiles. • **Conclusion:** No snakes have fur.
• **Premise 1:** All kittens are playful. • **Premise 2:** Some pets are kittens. • **Conclusion:** Some pets are playful.	• **Premise 1:** No homework is fun. • **Premise 2:** Some reading is homework. • **Conclusion:** Some reading is not fun.

Notice that in each case, the syllogism shares in common a single term between the premises. From left to right, top to bottom, these are "animals," "reptiles," "kittens," and "homework." Also observe that the content of the premises is largely irrelevant to the conclusions they yield. That is to say, statements like "all kittens are playful" or "no homework is fun" are subjective and impossible to adequately substantiate. However, if you accept the validity of the premises, you have no right to disagree with the conclusion because syllogistic reasoning (when applied according using the rule of non-contradiction) is airtight. That's right, it's 100% perfect. Unfortunately, premises are always based on induction which is susceptible to error.

Finally, you should observe among these four syllogisms that outcomes can be calculated based on how groups are defined: "all" (total group), "no/none" (total group), and "some" (partial group). Again, note that this calculation holds true regardless of the content of the premises, thus:

- all/all = all
- all/none or none/all = none
- all/some or some/all = some
- none/some or some/none = some

You should use these principles of deductive logic to inform or persuade your audience wherever possible, keeping in mind that the soundness of your conclusions are wholly dependent upon the inductive validity of your premises and the proper application of the principles of deduction, most notably the rule of non-contradiction.

Exercise (Syllogisms): Solve for the following syllogisms and then create your own logical syllogism in the space beneath.

No fish have toes.

All trout are fish.

Therefore:

No lazy people finish college

Some students finish college

Therefore:

All of the good students have red hair

Some of the good students live on campus

Therefore:

Your syllogism:

Additional Space:

Causal Logic

Though related to induction and deduction, **causal logic** is also important to consider independently. Causation occurs when one or more events, variables, and/or factors result in one or more additional events, variables, and/or factors. For example, if I were to drain all of the oil out of my car before starting it up and driving it around, it would result in severe damage to the engine. The causal sequence of events would include: (1) draining the oil, (2) starting the engine, and (3) driving the car. The resulting sequence of events would include: (1) a loss of oil pressure, (2) a loss of viscosity (the layer of oil between the parts of an engine), (3) intense friction and physical damage to the engine, (4) engine seizure (the engine would cease to function).

Even in this simple example, it is important to note that the cause/effect relationship is divisible and complex. I could summarize just by saying "If I started my car without oil, it would ruin the engine," but that would not account for all of the mediating conditions actually responsible for ruining the engine. In this particular case, that's probably sufficient because the relationship between starting a car without oil and damage to the engine is so clear; however, in more complex and contested cause/effect claims, more details are necessary because the relationship between events, variables, and/or factors is less clear.

Let's say, though, that someone did contest the causal proposition that starting my car without oil would ruin the engine. We could test the hypothesis by starting a bunch of engines without any oil in them and observing the results. Unfortunately, this wouldn't give us any insight into the chain of events responsible for engine failure, just that engine failure is extremely likely to occur. For a stronger causal argument, what we need is a warrant (a piece of evidence connecting cause and effect). In this example, the specific **warrant** is the breakdown in viscosity between engine parts (i.e., pistons, piston rings, cylinders, etc.) that is responsible for the intense friction, scraping, and gouging that would ultimately destroy the engine. Oil viscosity is the critical link connecting (1) lack of oil in a running engine to (2) engine damage. When constructing or examining cause/effect arguments, you should always be aware of this critical link called the warrant.

When cause/effect arguments lack a warrant, they are susceptible to the logical fallacy (mistake) known as "post hoc ergo propter hoc" (after, therefore because of). Just because one event happens after another event doesn't mean the two events are causally related. For example, if I eat a hamburger and then feel ill the next day, it might be due to the hamburger, but it also might not. It's hard to say what the relationship is between the hamburger and my illness without further investigation of the ingredients used in the hamburgers that were served and of other factors related to me.

Finally, when considering cause/effect relationships, we also have to think about **necessary** and **sufficient** conditions. Necessary conditions are conditions that are required for a particular result, but may not be the only conditions required for that result. Sufficient conditions, however, represent all that is required for a particular result to occur. Using the oil/engine sequence above, for example, notice how "(1) draining the oil" is a *necessary* condition for destroying the engine in this way, but it is not a *sufficient* condition. Draining the oil will not harm the engine, so long as the engine is not started while it is empty of oil. In fact, draining the oil is an important part of routine car maintenance.

Exercise (Causal Logic): For each of the following social problems, try to identify at least one causal factor. For one of the problems below, define the "warrant" and provide a detailed explanation of the connection between the social problem and its cause.

1. High rates of infant mortality in developing nations.

2. High murder rates in U.S. cities.

3. Low rates of college completion among working-class Americans.

4. High rates of teenage pregnancy in poor communities.

5. High rates of homelessness among the mentally ill.

6. Full-time employees who live in poverty and qualify for public assistance.

7. Prison overcrowding in the United States and the cost of incarceration to taxpayers.

8. High school graduates who are underprepared for college.

9. Reduced access to healthy food in poor neighborhoods.

10. Low voter turnout and low levels of civic engagement among U.S. citizens.

OTHER IMPORTANT LOGICAL PRINCIPLES

In several of the following subsections, you will notice some statements that appear like algebra equations. Don't worry if algebra isn't your strong suit, because these are only used as a means of reducing the **ambiguity of language** (uncertainty that leads to misinterpretation) and clarifying in symbolic terms the precise meaning of a particular statement. If applicable, you should subject key statements in your own speech (e.g., Central Idea, Main Ideas, and Conclusive Statement) to these methods of symbolic manipulation. Not all of these tools will apply to every speech, but they are still important to the cultivation of logical thinking, which is what you should always strive for in your presentation.

Leibniz's Law (Indiscernibility of the Identical) states that things are identical if everything that can be said of one thing can also be said of the other. Consider the following

- X=X (This is taken as a given.)
- If X=Y, then Y=X.
- If X=Y, and Y=Z, then X=Z.
- X is not not X.
- If X=Y, then (not X) = (not Y)

Let's explore the consequences of this using the classic syllogism about Socrates' mortality:

> - **Premise 1:** Socrates is a man.
> - **Premise 2:** All men are mortal.
> - **Conclusion:** Socrates is mortal.

X = X

 » Socrates (X) is Socrates (X)

If X=Y, and Y=Z, then X=Z

 » Socrates (X) is a man (Y). All men (Y) are mortal (Z). Socrates (X) is mortal (Z).

Leibniz's Law takes things a step further, noting the following logical extensions from the list above:

» If all men (X) are mortal (Y), then there are no men (not X) who are not mortal (not Y).

X is not not X.

» If Socrates is mortal (X), then Socrates is also not immortal (not not X).

If X = Y, then (not Y) = (not X)

» If Socrates (X) is a man (Y), then if you are not a man (not Y), you are not Socrates (not X).

REDUCTIO AD ABSURDUM

Consistent with the rule of non-contradiction, reductio ad absurdum begins with the assumption that a given statement is true and examines its interaction with other true statements to test its validity. If a contradiction arises, then the initial statement must be false.

For example, the statement "the earth is flat" would be accepted as true, but extended for the purpose of examining what the real consequences would be of having a flat earth. If the earth were flat, setting off in a single direction and staying true to that course should reveal one of two possible outcomes: (1) an infinite expanse of earth, or (2) a boundary where earth ends. Because neither of these statements are true, we must assume that the initial statement is false.

One drawback of *reductio ad absurdum* is that it relies upon Leibniz's axiom of the "excluded middle" (see below) which means that all statements are either true or false (X or not X). So, for example, if a statement's opposite is rejected as false, than the statement itself must be considered true. Not all statements lend themselves well to this format.

For a persuasive speech, any claim you make, including Central Idea, Proposition, and Conclusive Statement, should be subjected to the reductio ad absurdum method. Most of the time we do this automatically, but for public presentations, it's a good idea to make sure by consciously mapping out how your claim interacts with other widely accepted facts about the world.

PROVING AN ARGUMENT

In a geometric proof, statements are given which lead step-by-step to a conclusion, and each step requires a reason or "proof" to be provided. This method of reasoning can be employed effectively in informative speeches because it adheres to the principle of

complexity: simple information precedes and constructs complex information. It's also effective for persuasive arguments because it demands verification of each proposition that the speaker makes.

EMBEDDED MEANINGS

As noted at the start of this subsection, some of these logic exercises are intended only as a way of reducing ambiguity and the likelihood of misinterpretation for a given statement. The statement that follows is broken down into pieces and analyzed in terms of the meaning of its component parts. The value of doing this is that it provides maximum control over the meaning of your words and reduces the chances of misinterpretation or unintended implication.

DISSECTING A STATEMENT

Consider the following statement:

Some good teachers help some bright children read some simple books.

What do we know and what can we logically say about this statement? The list below identifies all the meanings that can be extracted from this simple sentence.

1. Some teachers are good.

2. Some teachers are not good.

(If all teachers were good, the qualifier "good" would be unnecessary.)

3. Some children are bright.

4. Some children are not bright.

(If all children were bright, the qualifier "bright" would be unnecessary.)

5. Some books are simple.

6. Some books are not simple.

(If all books were simple, the qualifier "simple" would be unnecessary.)

7. Some good teachers help.

8. Some good teachers do not help.

(Some is a subset of all, so if "some" good teachers help, then some do not.)

9. Some bright children read.

10. Some bright children do not read.

(Some is a subset of all, so if "some" bright children read, then some do not.)

11. Some simple books are read.

12. Some simple books are not read (by bright children who were helped by good teachers).

(Some is a subset of all, so if "some" simple books are read, then some are not.)

Meanings that cannot be extracted from the statement above include:

1. No teachers who are not good help.

(The statement does not implicate teachers who are "not good.")

2. No children who are not bright read.

(The statement does not implicate children who are "not bright.")

3. No books that are not simple are read.

(The statement does not implicate books that are "not simple.")

4. Some teachers are bad.

(The use of a particular term doesn't implicate its opposite.)

5. Some children are dumb.

(The use of a particular term doesn't implicate its opposite.)

6. Some books are complicated.

(The use of a particular term doesn't implicate its opposite.)

Perhaps some of these meanings resonate with your personal experience, but they are in no way implied by the logic of the sentence above.

Can you dissect the central idea of your speech this way?

Exercise (Dissecting Statements): Use what you've learned above to dissect the following statement: "Only good teachers help bright students read books."

TRUTH TABLES

The purpose of a truth table is to determine which conditions are necessary for a particular statement to be considered true. For example, consider these two potential conditions:

1. The door is closed.

The door is closed = (p)	The door is locked = (q)
T	T
T	F
F	T
F	F

The door is closed (p)	The door is locked (q)	The door is closed AND locked (p & q)
T	T	T
T	F	F
F	T	F
F	F	F

The door is closed (p)	The door is locked (q)	The door is closed OR locked (p & q)
T	T	T
T	F	T
F	T	T
F	F	F

The door is closed (p)	The door is locked (q)	The door is closed NOT locked (p & q)
T	T	F
T	F	T
F	T	F
F	F	F

A tautology is a statement that is true under all conditions. The following is an example of a tautology:

The door is closed (p1)	The door is locked (p2)	The door is closed NOT locked (p1 & q2)
T	F	T
F	T	T

Can you build a truth table out of your proposition?

Paradoxes & Fallacies

A paradox is a statement that violates the rule of non-contradiction of terms. A classic example is "This sentence is false." The truth of the statement is rejected by the statement itself. A paradox is, thus, impossible to interpret logically. However, obstacles to logical reasoning are not always as clear as an obvious paradox. More often, they take the form of fallacies, which are more subtle barriers to systematic thinking. The following list is based on the one compiled by Bradley Dowden for the Internet Encyclopedia of Philosophy. Define

Exercise (Fallacies): Divide the list of fallacies among your classmates. For homework, look up your fallacy (or fallacies), read it, and write a definition using your own language. Do not just copy definitions from the website. Use the following URL as a reference: http://www.iep.utm.edu/fallacy/#H6v

1. Ad Hominem

2. Ad Baculum

3. Ad Consequentiam

4. Ad Crumenum

5. Ad Hoc

6. Ad Ignorantiam

7. Ad Misericordiam

8. Ad Populum

9. Ad Verecundiam

10. Affirming the Consequent

11. The False Dilemma

12. Ambiguity

13. Anecdotal Evidence

14. Argumentum Consensus Gentium

15. Circular Reasoning

16. Red Herring

17. Socrites Fallacy

18. Presupposing

8. Ad Populum

9. Ad Verecundiam

10. Affirming the Consequent

11. The False Dilemma

12. Ambiguity

13. Anecdotal Evidence

14. Argumentum Consensus Gentium

15. Circular Reasoning

16. Red Herring

17. Socrites Fallacy

18. Presupposing

30. Formal Fallacy

31. Gambler's Fallacy

32. Groupthink

33. Hedging Your Bet

34. The Hooded Man

35. Reification

36. Non Sequitur

37. Inductive Conversion

38. Intensional

39. Logical Chopping (Doublespeak)

40. Lying

41. Modal

42. Oversimplification

43. Perfectionist

44. Prosecutor's Fallacy

45. Quantifier Shift

46. Out of Context

47. Scapegoating

48. Self-Fulfilling Prophecy

49. Sharpshooter's Fallacy

50. Style vs. Substance

51. Subjectivist Fallacy

52. Superstition

53. Tokenism

54. Untestability

55. Willful ignorance

56. Wishful Thinking

Ethical Reasoning

According to the Association of American Colleges and Universities, the definition of ethical reasoning is "reasoning about right and wrong human conduct" (Ethical Reasoning Value Rubric, Definition). In general, the purpose of ethical reasoning is to "act so as to help rather than harm other persons or sentient creatures" (Paul & Elder, p. 17), thus we can consider helping to be "right" and harming to be "wrong." Of course, in many contexts where ethical reasoning comes into play, what is helpful or harmful isn't always immediately very clear. As a way of confronting this ambiguousness, ethical reasoning demands consideration and evaluation of "values," "perspectives," "social contexts," and "alternative actions."

- **Values** were previously defined as "deeply held personal judgments about right and wrong." Values may be transmitted to us during our formative years by figures of authority (e.g., parents, teachers, mentors), or by formative personal experiences. It is, of course, possible for values to be good or bad based on the above stated purpose. Bad values do harm and good values are values that provide help.

- **Perspectives** address the fact that any ethical question or dilemma requires us to consider not only our own point of view (including attitudes, beliefs, and values), but the perspectives of others as well. Naturally, this does not mean that bad values (values that do harm) should be considered valid. However, the reason as to why bad values are bad should be made clear through evidence and the logical reasoning structures provided above.

- **Social Context** considers the importance of human interaction and culture in ethical reasoning. Our personal values are not ours alone, they are the product of human social interaction and the collective production of meaning common to all cultures. Therefore, when considering ethical reasoning and action, we need to consider the context under which values are produced.

- **Alternative Actions** are the heart of the ethical reasoning process. For harmfulness to be reduced and helpfulness to be increased, action needs to take place based on a reasoning process that considers values, perspectives, social context, and possible courses of action. In weighing alternative courses of action, the potential consequences of each need to be carefully considered based on the purpose of ethical reasoning: to help rather than harm other persons or sentient creatures. Here again, evidence and the logical reasoning

Richard Paul and Linda Elder (2013) have developed the following eight-step plan for tackling ethical questions:

1. Considering my own rights and needs as well as those of others in this situation, my [ethical] purpose should be:

2. The key ethical question(s) I am trying to answer is/are:

3. The most important information I will need to answer this ethical question is:

4. The key ethical concepts and principles that should guide my thinking are:

5. The main assumptions I am using in reasoning through this ethical issue are:

6. The points of view I need to consider before coming to conclusions about this ethical issue are:

7. The main inferences/conclusions I am coming to in reasoning through this ethical issue are:

8. If I come to the conclusions stated in number seven above, some of the important implications for myself and others are:

Exercise (Ethical Reasoning): Consider the following scenario: You are preparing a speech of persuasion for presentation at a professional convention and it's your task to convince your audience (a group of potential customers) that your product is superior to a competing product offered by another company. In the process of reviewing data gathered by competent independent researchers, you determine that under some circumstances, your product doesn't perform as well, but in others it performs better. Reason through this ethical problem by answering each of Paul and Elder's eight questions listed previously.

Chapter Five:
The Plot Thickens

In this chapter you will learn about the proper format and function of the central idea and main points of your speech. You will also be provided strategies for organizing your main points, methods for delivering your speech, and instructions for devising an outline with an effective introduction and conclusion

Developing Your Central Idea and Main Points

The **central idea** and **main points** of your speech are collectively referred to as the **blueprint,** because they provide a plan for the speech's structure. As previously described, the central idea takes on different forms in the context of narrative, informative, and persuasive speeches.

Unless the speech is given exclusively for the purpose of entertainment (e.g., telling a story for the sake of the story itself), the central idea of a narrative speech is the "lesson" of the story. This lesson might be moral, philosophical, or practical in nature and it usually comes at the end of the story so that the assertion has resonance with what the audience just heard. A speaker might use a story as testimony to endorse a personal value or belief. In such situations, the central idea is not proven or demonstrated, it is interpreted through identification with the speaker. Speeches like this rely very heavily on the ethos and pathos dimensions of persuasion discussed previously. For example, recall the story "Sensei Chinen" under the section "Our Stories" at the beginning of this book. The central idea of that speech is as follows: "So as a student I learned the value of courage, and as a teacher I learned the value of intensity. Thus, as you finish this course, I encourage you to go forward learning courageously and teaching intensely." Central ideas often come at the end of narrative speeches so that the audience has an opportunity to consider the meaning of the story before it is revealed by the speaker.

Informative and persuasive central ideas come in forms specific to the respective purposes of the informative and persuasive speech. Central ideas for informative speeches are **lessons,** while central ideas for persuasive speeches are **propositions.**

Lessons deal with implied questions like "how is something done?" (a speech of demonstration), "why is something happening or why did something happen?" (a speech of fact-based causality), or "what does something or someone mean?" (a speech of interpretative analysis). Other questions, including "who, where, and when" are also possible, but often overlap with these more complex questions. Here are some central ideas that apply to each of these categories:

- **Demonstration:** "I will demonstrate how to brew beer."

- **Causality**: "I will explain why public disinvestment in higher education is responsible for the college student loan crisis."

- **Interpretation:** "I will present an interpretive analysis of the television program *Sons of Anarchy*."

Propositions come in three forms: "propositions of fact," "propositions of value," and "propositions of policy." Propositions of fact are central ideas which propose a statement about something that is true about the world. Propositions of value are central ideas about widely applicable notions of right or wrong. Propositions of policy are central ideas that propose a solution to a collective problem.

- **Fact:** Corporations benefit from public assistance programs.

- **Value:** Environmental protection is the responsibility of every citizen.

- **Policy:** We should reclassify drug addiction as a mental health issue to reduce the problem of prison overcrowding.

Now that we've established the function and form of the central idea, let's focus on **main points**. Your main points in an informative speech should serve to clarify through definition, description, and/or explanation, whereas in a persuasive speech they should serve to persuade through evidence, reasoning, and logic.

- **Definition:** A definition represents an exact, agreed upon description of meaning for a particular term or concept.

- **Description:** A description refers to the translation of one person's sensory experience of someone (a person or people), something (an object), somewhere (a place), and/or something that happened (an event) to another person or people.

- **Explanation:** An abstract description concerning the basic nature or essence of something intended to foster understanding in another person or people.

- **Reasoning:** The process of drawing conclusions from evidence.

- **Logic**: The abstract set of rules for thinking that guide reasoning.

STRATEGIES FOR ORGANIZING YOUR SPEECH

Main points should be organized based on one of the following strategies: chronological, spatial, topical, or problem/solution. Next, we'll consider each of these strategies in terms of how they might be used to elaborate upon a central idea.

- **Chronological:** The chronological strategy is borrowed from narrative storytelling where events follow from one another creating suspense and leading to a climax event from which the lesson or moral of the story is drawn In a narrative speech that proposes a value based on the speaker's personal experience, the story would likely be divided into events and each event would serve as a main point leading to the climax.

- **Spatial:** The spatial strategy uses place, space, geography, or location as a tool of organization. If, for example you were organizing an informative speech that identified zip code as predictor of poverty, you might allow spatial relationships between cities, boroughs, districts, towns, and counties to develop your argument.

- **Topical:** The topical strategy lets you use your own logic to organize topics in cases where none of the others are appropriate. For example, in the speech interpreting *Sons of Anarchy*, you might use specific character representations as a means of structuring the speech.

- **Problem/Solution**: The problem/solution strategy divides the body of the speech into pairs of main points: one to describe problems and the other to offer solutions. Notice the relationship this strategy has to causal logic (see Chapter Four: Logic, Reasoning, Evidence, and Ethics) and to informative speeches of fact-based causality. The best way to solve a problem is to be aware of the factors that cause the problem. "We should reclassify drug addiction as a mental health issue to reduce the problem of prison overcrowding," stated above, could easily be organized according to problem/solution. The first main point would describe the problem of prison overcrowding, its consequences, and its causes, and the second main point would offer reclassification of drug addiction as a solution and describe the consequence of this change.

- **Monroe's Motivated Sequence**: This strategy is a variation of the problem solution arrangement wherein the audience is offered a "need" (a problem), a "satisfaction" (a solution to the problem), "visualization" scenarios where the problem is solved and/or not solved, and "action" where the audience is called upon to do something to enact the satisfaction/solution. For an excellent example of the practical use of Monroe's Motivated Sequence, please view Adichie's speech "The Danger of a Single Story," in Appendix C. Persuasive TED Talks and observe how in the last part of her speech, she continuously poses the question "what if " to her audience as a prompt for getting them to imagine alternative ways of thinking.

CONSTRUCTING AND USING AN OUTLINE

NARRATIVE SPEECH OUTLINE

To prepare the outline for your narrative speech, take the following elements into consideration. Every piece of information you include should fall into one of these six categories. Transportation and background are usually placed at the beginning of the story, while climax and re-entry appear at the end. Events and transitions occur throughout the story.

Transportation: Do you have a strategy for bringing your audience into the world of the story?

Background: Do you include the necessary names, dates, summaries, and descriptions of persistent conditions so that your audience isn't confused about the context of your story?

Events: Does each event include a person who is located in a setting where one or more actions take place?

Transitions: Does your story move smoothly through the events by refocusing the audience's attention with transitional phrases?

Climax: Is the story organized around a central event where the opposing forces of the narrative ultimately meet each other?

Re-entry: Do you provide appropriate verbal and/or nonverbal cues to indicate the conclusion of the story and avoid an abrupt ending?

INFORMATIVE SPEECH OUTLINE

Use the following guidelines to prepare your informative speech outline:

Attention: The very first statement of the speech intended to gain the audience's attention. This statement should be clearly related to the central idea and it shouldn't overwhelm the forthcoming message of the speech. Often, attention statements take the form of intriguing questions, surprising facts or observations, shocking measurements, or powerful quotations.

Central Idea: The statement which explains what the **lesson** of the informative speech is going to be about.

Importance: The statement of importance explains why the knowledge to be gained through the speech is important to the speaker and should be important to the audience.

Credibility: The statement of credibility is intended to demonstrate the competence of the speaker and win the trust of the audience.

Preview of Main Points: The preview of main points is a list of points that will be elaborated upon in the body of the speech. This preview is only intended as a "table of contents" or "roadmap" for the rest of the speech, it is not the place to elaborate on the points themselves.

In an informative speech, main points can be organized according to the strategies presented in the section titled "Strategies for Organizing Your Speech," which includes chronological, spatial, and topical. However, the principle of **complexity** should be considered when organizing a speech based on topic. This means that the simplest or most basic pieces of information should come before the more complex and advanced information.

Transition: The first transition combines verbal and nonverbal cues that the speaker is moving into the body of the speech.

Elaboration of Main Points: The main points are an extension of the central idea. Their purpose in the context of the informative speech is to explain, describe, and/or define the lesson as fully as possible. The main points must be supported by logic, reasoning, evidence, and research wherever possible.

Transition: The second transition combines verbal and nonverbal cues that the speaker is moving into the conclusion of the speech.

Recap of Main Points: Similar to the preview described above, the recap of main points is a list of points that have been elaborated upon in the body of the speech. Just as in the preview, the recap is not intended to elaborate upon the points or introduce new information.

Restatement of the Central Idea: The statement intended to remind the audience of the lesson.

Conclusive Statement: The conclusive statement is the very last statement of the speech and should be both concise and memorable.

PERSUASIVE SPEECH OUTLINE

Use the following guidelines to prepare your persuasive speech outline:

Attention: The very first statement of the speech intended to gain the audience's attention. This statement should be clearly related to the central idea and it shouldn't overwhelm the forthcoming message of the speech. Often, attention statements take the form of intriguing questions, surprising facts or observations, shocking measurements, or powerful quotations.

Central Idea: In a persuasive speech, the central ideal is the **proposition** (statement that the speaker intends for the audience to accept). This may be a proposition of action, fact, policy, or value.

Importance: The statement of importance explains why it is important to the speaker that the audience accepts the proposition offered and why accepting the proposition should be important to the audience.

Credibility: The statement of credibility is intended to demonstrate the competence of the speaker and win the trust of the audience.

Preview of Main Points: The preview of main points is a list of points that will be elaborated upon in the body of the speech. This preview is only intended as a "table of contents" or "roadmap" for the rest of the speech, it is not the place to elaborate on the points themselves.

In a persuasive speech, evidence should dictate the order of presentation for the main points. As noted in the section titled "Strategies for Organizing Your Speech," chronological, spatial, topical, and problem/solution strategies might be employed. However, in addition to accounting for hierarchy of knowledge (as in according to strength, since not all points are based on equally convincing evidence. In general, the principle of **recency** should be employed, wherein the strongest or most convincing points are saved for last. Alternatively, **primacy** may be used with skeptical or otherwise unreceptive audiences. Primacy places the most compelling evidence upfront in an attempt to capture the interest and imagination of resistant listeners and get them to at least entertain the proposition. **Monroe's Motivated Sequence** is another, more specialized strategy, which employs visualization as a persuasive technique.

Transition: The first transition combines verbal and nonverbal cues that the speaker is moving into the body of the speech.

Elaboration of Main Points: The main points are an extension of the proposition. Their purpose in the context of the persuasive speech is to provide evidence and an argument that supports the proposition as fully as possible. The main points must be supported by research (see Chapter Four), evidence (the information gained from research), and logical reasoning (the use of evidence in forming a conclusion). Transition: The second transition combines verbal and nonverbal cues that the speaker is moving into the conclusion of the speech.

Recap of Main Points: Similar to the preview described above, the recap of main points is a list of the arguments that have been elaborated upon in the body of the speech. Just as in the preview, the recap is not intended to elaborate upon the argument or introduce new evidence.

Restatement of the Central Idea: This statement is a restatement of the proposition.

Conclusive Statement: The conclusive statement is the very last statement of the speech and should be both concise and memorable. If appropriate, the conclusive statement should contain a "call to action" where the speaker urges the audience to act upon the proposition.

Chapter Six:
Show & Tell

Nonverbal Communication and Delivery

There are seven aspects of delivery:

Posture: Posture refers to the way you stand in front of the room and it is vitally important to projecting confidence and enhancing your credibility. Confident posture means having your feet about shoulder-width apart, your back straight, and your shoulders square.

Gestures: Gesture refers to how you use your hands to communicate throughout the speech. Regulatory gestures help control and telegraph the pace of your speech and should be used persistently throughout your presentation. Demonstrative gestures function to illustrate physical features by approximating them manually. Emphatic gestures are used to conduct the speaker's emotions and to serve as the equivalent of a nonverbal exclamation.

Facial Expressions: The face is a very subtle conductor of emotion. During a speech, we should strive to present an emotional state that is consistent with the subject matter. Because the biological mechanisms behind facial expressions are complex, it's best to "get into character" before presenting a speech, so that the expressions you project to the audience are consistent with your message.

Eye Contact: It's critically important to look at your audience when you speak to them. With very large audiences, it's appropriate to gaze in the general direction of different parts of the audience, but for most speaking events you'll encounter it's necessary to look specific audience members in the eyes in order to engage them. Therefore, you should strive for individualized, sustained eye contact where you share your attention with different members of the audience throughout the room as you speak.

Paralanguage: Even though paralanguage refers to the way you use your voice, it's technically nonverbal communication because it deals with the delivery of words and not the words themselves. Good paralanguage should include a lot of variety to captivate interest and increase comprehension.

Proxemics: Your movement throughout the room during your presentation is called proxemics. Proxemics can be used successfully to engage different parts of the room in conjunction with eye contact and posture, but it can also be used to facilitate transitions between events (in a narrative speech) or between main points (in informative and persuasive speeches).

Chronemics: As you might have guessed from the prefix "chron" as in "chronological," chronemics is about how you use time in your speech. A common error is rapid speech, which impedes the audience's ability to keep up and comprehend the message of the speech. However, chronemics also encompasses pacing, which refers to the appropriate use of pauses throughout the speech. Like paralanguage, chronemics should include a lot of variety. New and complicated information requires more time than information the audience is already familiar with.

INCORPORATING PRESENTATION AIDS

The primary purpose of presentation aids is to help the audience better understand the topic.

- Options for choosing a presentation aid:
    - »» You or another person in physical demonstrations.
    - »» A smart board, chalkboard, or dry-erase board for writing or drawing.
    - »» An object or model.
    - »» Digital images, video clips, and audio clips.
    - »» Presentation software.
- Requirement for preparing the presentation aid:
- »» Devote time to building your presentation aid.
    - »» Make it large enough for the entire audience to see.
    - »» Be in control of the presentation aid at all times.
    - »» Keep it as simple as possible while still conveying the intended meaning.
    - »» Limit the number of aids you are using throughout the presentation.

- »» Show the aid only when you are referring to it.

- »» Maintain eye contact with the audience throughout the speech. Don't focus your attention on the aid. You should already be intimately familiar with it.

- »» Do not pass any presentation aid throughout the audience during the speech, as it will distract the audience from your speech.

- »» Practice with presentation aids beforehand to maintain timing and ensure proper functioning.

• Reminders

- »» It's always possible for technical difficulties or accidents to occur with the presentation aid, so be prepared to improvise.

- »» Have a back-up file for all electronic presentation aids (e.g., external harddrive, FTP, e-mail message attachment).

- »» Be prepared to deliver your speech without any presentation aid if necessary.

Chapter Seven: Assignments

This chapter contains assignment options and descriptions for narrative, informative, and persuasive speeches. Review Chapter Three: A Tale of Three Speeches for a recap of these categories. (All assignments are subject to modification by the instructor of the course.)

Assignment (Folk Tale Speech): A folk tale is a story originating from the general public that often lacks authorship credit and is intended to convey a moral lesson. Choose a folktale from any cultural tradition and create an outline of it by identifying (1) the series of events, (2) the linkages between them, (3) the climax event, and (4) any relevant background information. Be prepared to perform this folktale in front of the class. For an example of how to identify the different components of your folk tale, go to Appendix A, Analysis of Folktales.

Chapter Seven: Assignments

Assignment (Speech of Demonstration): Consider your experience, interests, and talents for performing a specific task, and prepare an informative speech that shares this knowledge with the audience in the form of a lesson. Your topic should also take into account audience, context, and environment (Chapter Two). Make certain to fact-check your information with research (Chapter Four) and make use of chronological and/or spatial organization (Chapter Five). Outline your speech below.

Chapter Seven: Assignments

*Note: Complete the "Proposition of Fact" Speech in conjunction with this assignment.

Assignment (Speech of Causality): Revisit your responses to the causal logic exercise in Chapter Four. Using one of these topics, or a new one approved by your instructor, develop a lesson that teaches your audience about the causes of a particular social problem. Gather evidence and evaluate your cause/effect relationship according to the rules of logic and reasoning described in Chapter Four.

Chapter Seven: Assignments

Assignment (Speech of Analysis): Analyze the folk tale you presented in your first assignment according to its moral lesson or value system. Then develop a lesson about the moral meaning of the story. Begin by summarizing the story and providing a historical, regional, and cultural context. Follow up by providing previous interpretations of the story, and, lastly, provide your own informed analysis based on character and narrative outcomes. Provide thorough documentation or evidence at each step.

Chapter Seven: Assignments

Assignment (Proposition of Fact): All persuasive speeches are based on propositions of fact: statements that claim some truth about the world. It is in the interpretation of these proposed facts, however, that one finds the real art of persuasion. Identify the most important fact for your Speech of Causality assignment and provide well-documented evidence in support of it.

Chapter Seven: Assignments

Assignment (Proposition of Value): All of us have a value system that we've developed and refined over the course of our lifetimes. Take some time to consider a value that defines who you are (e.g., courage, wisdom, strength, fairness, loyalty, perseverance, equality, assertiveness, or something completely different). Once you've arrived at this formative value, look back upon the episodes and events of your life and try to determine if there is a particular series of events that led you to adopt this value. Alternatively, you might start by considering an important episode in your life and think about what value it taught you that you hold today. In the space provided below, develop a value statement and provide a breakdown of the events that led you to this value. For an example of this assignment, look at the "Sensei Chinen" story under the section Our Stories at the beginning of the book.

Chapter Seven: Assignments

Chapter Seven: Assignments

Assignment (Proposition of Policy): Refer back to the causal logic exercise and to your Speech of Causality assignment. Based on these, formulate a policy solution to the underlying social problem. A policy is a collective course of action intended to solve a social problem. In formulating your proposition of policy, be certain to explain how your solution addresses each of the causes you explained in your Speech of Causality. Provide thorough evidence for each aspect of your policy to explain why it is necessary to be effective.

Chapter Eight: Tricks of the Trade

Practicing Effectively

It's impossible to underestimate the importance of practice to the effectiveness of your speech. In movies and on television, impromptu (spontaneous) speeches are sometimes dramatized, as when a speaker stands up before a crowded room with notes that, after some hesitation, are crumpled and discarded in favor of "speaking from the heart." That is never a good idea. Experiencing an emotion or having an idea is not sufficient for giving a good speech. Believe it or not, even expertise gained from years of study on a subject is not enough to guarantee a good speech. It's possible to know something very well and fail horribly in the act of attempting to articulate it. Let me offer two brief illustrations:

- Part of the requirements for completing my doctoral degree included a public presentation of preliminary research findings from my dissertation project. When it came time for me to present, I had been a student of communication for ten years and working on my dissertation for almost two. I felt confident that I was an "expert" on the subject I was studying. However, when I went to actually present my work, I stumbled about halfway through and never completely regained my confidence during that presentation. Fortunately, the audience was able to look past my poor delivery and appreciate the underlying ideas I was offering, but I was stunned at my poor performance. How could this have happened after all my work? The answer to this question is: because all of my work was aimed at learning something, not about teaching something. To teach something, you have to do more than just know it, you have to be able to present what you know clearly and in a way that the audience is capable of understanding. That is, you must be able to summarize and reduce the complexity of your ideas. Thus, as deeply involved as I was with the work I was doing, I was in no condition to present without first disengaging from it and summarizing what I had already done.

- Perhaps this effect is more drastically illustrated in the process of learning a new language. About four years ago, I decided to start learning German for my own personal curiosity and satisfaction. I completed the Rosetta Stone program and downloaded many language learning applications to my smartphone and tablet to make practice as frequent and easy as possible. I also read and copied children's books that were written in German and practiced chatting online through language learning websites like LiveMocha and SharedTalk. One day, I thought it would be interesting to experiment with a Skype chat, but when I logged on and greeted my German-speaking partner, I quickly realized how unprepared I was. Unlike my dissertation, however, I could easily identify the problem this time. Despite the fact that I could read (basic) text rather well and even understand speech that was clear and slow, I still couldn't produce the language orally because **decoding** (how we make sense of speech) and encoding (how we create speech) are two different brain functions. I was good at **decoding,** but bad at encoding.

What you should take away from these examples is an understanding that to present an effective extemporaneous speech, you must not only adequately prepare the content; you must also be able to perform and articulate your speech effectively. Just because you've "decoded" a lot of research doesn't mean you'll be able to competently "encode" it into a cohesive speech.

WRITING AND REVISING AN OUTLINE

The following is a checklist for things to complete before you begin practicing your speech:

- Select a topic.
- Perform research.
- Formulate a central idea.
- Develop and organize main ideas.
- Develop an introduction and conclusion.
- Write the speech out in long form prose (i.e., write the speech out completely).
- Develop an outline based on what you've written, highlighting only the key points.
- Begin practicing your speech and revising your outline.
- Continue practicing your speech and revising your outline until it is time to present.

SIMULATING THE SPEAKING ENVIRONMENT

Environment plays a very important role in delivery. Think of a speech like a dramatic performance because, in every respect, it is. The space where you are presenting is your stage and the people before you are your audience. Just as actors might "block out" their movements on a stage, so must you block out locations, posture, gestures, timing, facial expressions, and eye contact as well. If you fail to practice your speech in a way that attempts to simulate the environment, you will feel awkward and uncomfortable in front of the room.

There are also several tools you should use to aid in rehearsing your speech:

- **Mirror**: Using a mirror is an excellent first step in practicing. Due to its instant feedback, the mirror lets you adjust (almost subconsciously) to develop the presentation you're most comfortable with. Even alone you may, at first, feel intensely self-conscious in front of the mirror. This is normal and it is essential to confront this feeling and fight through it. Remember that simply avoiding the way your presentation looks to your own eyes isn't going to make it appear any better to your audience. Get comfortable with your appearance and performance.

- **Video:** Once you've refined your performance in the mirror long enough so that you don't see any more obvious repeated mistakes or problems, you should move to video to gain a more analytical and disengaged perspective on your performance. Remember to frame your shot wide enough to permit movement, but tight enough so that eye contact and facial expressions are visible. Use the video to identify and correct weaknesses in your speech.

- **Stand-In Audience:** Once you're happy with your performance in front of the mirror and on video, it's time to find a small stand-in audience willing to provide some feedback for your speech. Choose people whom you trust to provide serious and honest feedback and provide them with some basic information before your speech, such as your general purpose (Inform, Persuade, or Entertain) and criteria from the evaluation form. You may even run off copies of the evaluation form for your standin audience to use as a means of providing feedback. Once you've presented your speech, incorporate any valid criticism into your delivery and/or outline.

JUST BEFORE THE SPEECH

In the moments prior to the speech, there is little to do. The work is already done and the success or failure of your presentation is almost predestined based on the investment you've made in preparation and practice. However, it's worth mentioning that rehearsing your introductory sentence, recounting your **blueprint** (central idea + main points), and taking a deep breath to calm your nerves can be very helpful. Meditation prior to the presentation of your speech (see Chapter Nine) is also highly recommended.

HELPFUL HINTS

Create notecards to help in extemporaneous delivery
- Select neutral colors to avoid distracting the audience and undermining speaker credibility.

- Use 3x5 notecards to make handling them easier and their appearance less conspicuous.

- Number your notecards.

- With the exception of direct quotations, don't write down full sentences. Limit your notes to key words so as to avoid reading.

- Highlight every other line to avoid losing your place.

- Using a different color or font, include nonverbal delivery cues on your notecards.

- If you have a presentation aid, include cues for when and how to incorporate it.

- Include time reminders.

- Include source information where it is appropriate.

Question-and-Answer Sessions
- After you've allowed a moment for your audience to applaud and reflect, ask if there are any questions.

- Anticipate questions that might be asked ahead of time so that you're more prepared to field them on the spot.

- If necessary, restate the question for the entire audience to hear.

- Answer the question in a way that's as direct and succinct as possible, without omitting important details or oversimplifying the answer.

- If no one asks you a question, stimulate the audience's interest with an interesting point you didn't have time to include.

- If you don't know the answer to a question, don't avoid and don't lie. Instead, offer to find the information and make certain to follow up.

Chapter Nine:
Relaxing in to Your Story: How to use Meditation to Control Speech Anxiety

You might be surprised that a book about public speaking has a chapter about meditation in it. The reason we included this chapter is that speaking in public is an extremely stressful experience for many people and can have a significant negative impact on the skills that you've developed throughout this course. Taken to the extreme, fear of public speaking can manifest as **Glossophobia** — "an irrational fear and avoidance of public speaking situations" which may hinder a person's career and social life.

Consider, for example, how fear of public speaking may inhibit opportunities in personal and professional settings. What if you were asked to give a conference presentation for work, but due to apprehension about standing up to speak in front of your peers, you decline? The likely consequence of this decision is that someone else will accept the offer and the opportunities that come along with it.

Also consider the likely scenario that, later in life, someone close to you dies. The ability to stand up before family, friends, coworkers, acquaintances, and strangers to deliver an effective eulogy can be a cathartic and therapeutic experience that reduces the grief associated with loss while honoring the person's memory and providing closure through narrative presentation.

Many other personal experiences can be added to these two examples as well, including wedding speeches, graduation speeches, victory speeches, retirement parties, particularly important birthday celebrations, and certain religious ceremonies.

A primary reason people fear public speaking is the social judgment implied by situation. The act of standing before an audience suggests that what you have to say is worth listening to insofar as it entertains, informs, or persuades the audience. It often carries with it the unspoken claim that the speaker is an expert on the subject as well. Failure, therefore, to prove worthy of the audience's time or to convince them of your expertise may represent an ego threat and manifest in the form of anxiety or feelings of inadequacy.

Furthermore, according to Aristotle, ethos (personal character) is a key component of effective speech, so it's little wonder that most people are apprehensive about public speaking, since the quality of their performance will be partly determined by the audience's evaluation of their personal character.

The first thing to realize in confronting speech anxiety is that some of it is healthy and can provide the fuel for an energetic speech performance. Eliminating all anxiety from speaking in public would make for delivery performances that were too bland and informal. The key is to harness your manageable anxiety and apply it to the task of developing a dynamic presentation style. This is where meditation techniques prove especially useful.

There are two general ways in which meditation can mitigate anxiety associated with public speaking: (1) reducing self-consciousness and (2) employing respiration as a means of physiological relaxation during speech. Both of these points will later be expanded upon, but it's presently sufficient to understand that a major focus and effect of meditation is the reduction of anxiety associated with **interpersonal perception management** (i.e., concern regarding other people's thoughts about us). Conversely, on the physiological side of things, breathing can be used as an effective tool for managing anxiety associated with public speaking.

One thing that meditation and speech share in common is the instrumental use of breathing. In speech, breath is the medium through which voice is produced. We breathe air into our lungs and expel it through our larynx, where it is manipulated through vocal cord contractions to produce speech sounds. Coordination of breath in speaking is vital to some central components of delivery, such as chronemics and paralanguage.

In meditation, breath is used as a focal point of concentration and a means of achieving psychological presence — a sensation of being situated in the "here and now."

DEFINITION OF MEDITATION

There are many different reasons why someone might meditate, ranging from religious practice to weight loss and the desire to quit smoking. Due to this extensive range of purpose, techniques and definitions can vary widely. In vast and simple terms, meditation is "a tool for relaxation" (Brown, 2012) or, even more basically, the act of "sitting quietly" (Sheridan, 2011). However, more meaningful definitions arise when we consider two opposite approaches to meditation: (1) **presence** and (2) **transcendence**.

Meditating to achieve transcendence might be done for many reasons, but they all have in common an initial step of turning inward to "facilitate adjustments of states of consciousness" (Davis, 1995/2011) or so-called "trance-states" (Paxson, 2008), wherein perception is altered and increased access to the unconscious mind enters our awareness.

In stark opposition, Tibetan Buddhist author, Pema Chödrön (2013) describes the essence of meditation as relaxing into the unknown of the present moment and remaining there with ourselves without applying judgment to the experience.

Notice how this second definition describes an approach to meditation that is highly applicable to public speaking. Like sports, music, art and any other process or performance based activity, success in public speaking is partially contingent upon the performer's ability to stay grounded and focused on the present moment. Meditation techniques that train us to remain present provide us with the skills necessary to focus on the ephemeral flow of our performance and reduce anxiety associated with interpersonal perceptions and perceived errors in execution.

None of this is to say, however, that transcendental meditation is without its value to our purpose of making better speeches. If presence meditation is helpful to executing good delivery and performance, transcendental meditation is equally helpful for gathering inspiration and developing content.

Followers of some religions practice transcendental meditation as a means of achieving altered states of consciousness in pursuit of spiritual fulfillment, but anyone can use these techniques in a strictly instrumental way to rid the mind of predisposed trains of thought and open new avenues for creative inspiration.

The primary difference between the two approaches is that presence meditation teaches us to look outward and ground ourselves in the "here and now," whereas transcendental meditation teaches us to look inward so we can transform our consciousness and cultivate repressed or unrealized mental potentials.

WHY MEDITATE?

Consistent with the transcendental approach described above, Roy Eugene Davis (1995/2011) explicitly claims that the purpose of meditation is to "facilitate adjustments of states of consciousness." In contrast, presence practitioners like Chödrön (2013) say that the reason for meditation is "to train the mind to reclaim its natural capacity to stay present." She also itemizes a list of other reasons for (presence) meditation, including steadfastness, clear-seeing, courage, being "awake" to our lives, and cultivating a "no big deal" attitude toward our challenges and triumphs. Though these are all worth learning and pursuing, some have more direct relevance to public speaking than others. Steadfastness, courage, and cultivation of the "no big deal" attitude are particularly salient.

Steadfastness and courage are complementary purposes insofar as "steadfastness" is defined as "a non-judgmental loyalty to one's own experience and "courage" is the ability to remain loyal (and non-judgmental) even in moments of severe anxiety or other emotional distress. Put simply, these qualities just mean learning how not to retreat (physically or emotionally) from tough experiences.

Cultivation of the so-called "no big deal" attitude is perhaps most useful in situations of public presentation. Chödrön intends it to be an expression of "humor and flexibility," and these are essential characteristics for our purposes.

Consider, for example, a speaker who's just about to step before the audience to start her speech. She has researched, organized and practiced thoroughly, but when she's on the stage, her presentation file fails to load on the computer. What should she do?

Most people in this situation (even those accustomed to public speaking) would panic. Their attention would become fixated on the computer file and the purpose of their speech would get lost in the mix. Afterward, they'd be plagued by frustration, embarrassment, and recurring thoughts about their missed opportunity. But is there another way to handle a situation like this one?

Practitioners of presence meditation would say yes. Through cultivation of the "no big deal" attitude, it's possible to salvage a situation like this one. After all, it's the file that was lost, not the presentation. The presentation is an abstraction, existing only in the gap of time that elapses during the interaction between audience and speaker, but the potential for the presentation exists in you.

Remember that in situations like this one, relatively little has actually changed. You still did your research, learned the material, organized the speech, and practiced carefully and correctly, so you can still give the speech. You may have to change some things on the fly (like adding descriptions or eliminating a sections that rely too heavily on the computer file), but you still have the knowledge and the audience. That's all you need. In fact, this might even be an opportunity to improvise and communicate even more directly with the audience, incorporating feedback and participation.

Notice how here in this example, steadfastness, courage, and the "no big deal" attitude all come together. In the ideal scenario, the speaker has the courage to stay with their stressful experience (*steadfastness*) and give the speech, all the while maintaining a flexible attitude and realizing that no particular part of the presentation is such a *big deal* that it can't be successful.

But even if the presentation doesn't work out the way it was imagined, it's still not the end of the world. Different speaking situations carry with them different opportunities, but it's still just one situation, and its overall level of importance in the grand scheme is extremely small, even insignificant. So relax, you can survive any speech.

How to Meditate

This section of the chapter, which deals with the practical instruction of meditation, is divided into three parts. We'll begin with some overall advice about starting and maintaining your meditation practice, move on to some technique recommendations, and finally offer some suggested procedures to incorporate those techniques.

Practice

All styles of meditation place an initial emphasis on making contact with the present moment (here and now), regardless of whether the ultimate purpose is to stay there or to explore the vast reaches of the internal mindscape. Therefore, it is important to establish a time and place for your meditation practice. Two common prescriptions in the literature on meditation are (1) practice first-thing in the morning and (2) practice for at least twenty minutes per day, every day.

In my own speech courses, we generally start off the session with a five-minute meditation, but this is only meant to establish an atmosphere while also refreshing students' post-meditative state. Twenty minutes of early practice is necessary for the five minute session to have full effect.

Another important concern is space. Where will you meditate and how will you use your body to occupy that space?

Depending on your purpose (presence or transcendence), you may have different answers to this question, so I'm not going to provide any hard and fast rules about this, just general suggestions.

1. Find a place in your home (or elsewhere) that you feel comfortable practicing.

2. Consider your meditation posture carefully. The overwhelmingly popular conclusion among meditation teachers is that one should practice meditation in a sitting position. There are even special seats to purchase for optimizing meditation posture. In contrast, though, there is an alternative school of thought that contends meditation can be effectively practiced lying down. This applies especially well to transcendental meditators. Another key difference in practice between presence and transcendence meditation is the gaze. Transcendentalists tend to meditate with their eyes closed, while those meditating on presence keep their eyes open.

Once time, space, and posture are squared away, it's time to consider **settling** prior to your meditation. This is where you prepare your ordinary orientation and consciousness so that it's susceptible to the meditative state. It generally involves two components: settling the body through systematic relaxation and settling the mind by gaining perspective on the emotional state.

The final common element to meditative practice is "letting go." This sounds like a simple instruction, but it's not. We are so used to hanging on to our ordinary state of consciousness that letting go is not initially easy. One can work on letting go with breathing exercises that require the meditator to focus on his or her respiration, using the exhaling breath as a tool to relax the grip on ordinary consciousness.

A final point on meditation practice is that it's not always a passive activity. Druidic meditation teacher, Nimue Brown writes that "meditation should be part of living, experiencing and acting, not separate from it." This is a very appealing possibility taken together with the act of public speaking. It stands to reason that if one could master the practice of meditation sufficiently to use it in active situations, then those activities could be performed calmly and with dramatically improved execution. Of course, to reach this level of comfort with the meditative state, it's necessary to be dedicated to daily practice.

TECHNIQUE

We've discussed the general framework of meditation practice, including time, space, posture, settling, and letting go. The next step is to fill in some specific detail describing meditation technique. Some techniques will apply more to presence meditation or transcendence meditation, and some will apply to both. However, as you read this, be aware that the most important thing is your own experience and that techniques are just tools intended to make us more susceptible to the shift in consciousness needed to enter a meditative state. Once this is achieved, techniques should be "discarded" so that direct experience with "pure meditation" can be achieved (Davis, 1995/2011).

Below, I will discuss techniques for posture, breathing, vocalization, movement, and guided narration.

Posture

As previously noted, the meditative position preferred by most teachers is a sitting posture. Specifically, Chödrön (2013) refers to the ideal posture as having an "open front," which means that you are looking straight ahead with your chin level to the ground. The spine should also be in straight alignment and the shoulders should be back, maintaining a balance and symmetry in your sitting position.

It's worthy of consideration that this 'ideal' posture bears a marked resemblance to the proper posture recommended for speech presentation delivery, so that it's possible to suggest that the practice of meditation in this position is also a form of practice that improves speaking posture and, thus, enhances confidence in front of the room.

To attain the 'open front' posture, Chödrön makes the following specific recommendations:

1. Seat: Use a stable, level base for your seat.

2. Hands: Rest your hands on your thighs, with the palms facing down.

3. Torso: The torso should be in an upright and relaxed position.

4. Eyes: Keep your eyes open during meditation.

5. Gaze: Look slightly downward without moving your head, neck or back.

6. Face: Permit the muscles in your face to go slack, eliminating all expression.

7. Legs: Cross your legs comfortably in front of you.

Let's provide some further explanation with respect to "seat/torso," "eyes/gaze," and "face," so you can fully understand why these techniques are being recommended for practicing meditation practicing meditation to reduce public speech anxiety.

Seat/Torso: Mediation instructors of Chödrön's tradition (Shamantha) commonly make similar recommendations as those above, but Nimue Brown (2012), coming from a Druidic perspective, places high emphasis on the center of gravity during meditation. Thus, it would seem especially important to select a stable, level seat and maintain an erect posture, because multiple traditions of meditation converge on this point.

Eyes/Gaze: As previously mentioned, presence and transcendence meditators differ here according to their aims. Presence meditators recommend keeping the eyes open and the gaze directed downward because their goal is to relax into the present moment and accept the conditions of the here and now. Closing one's eyes suggests an inward turning that is more consistent with transcendence. Some transcendental meditators enhance the inward turning experience even further by using a blindfold and earplugs to completely cancel out sight and sound. (Eliminating external sensory experience to facilitate internally produced altered states of consciousness is an effect that has been achieved in laboratory settings through the use of sensory deprivation chambers.)

Face: Allowing your facial muscles to completely slacken and eliminating all expression isn't just about achieving a state of relaxation. The cognitive effects of "muscle memory" will impede meditation through emotional associations with residual facial expressions. For example, having a slight smile or frown (or other expression) on your face will actually produce low levels of that emotion and make it more difficult to remain emotionally neutral during meditation.

Attempting to achieve a neutral facial expression through muscle relaxation may also assist in making the meditator more aware of his or her emotional state and how it's projected through expression. This is a valuable skill in managing impressions and rapport with an audience when speaking in public.

An Alternative Posture

For transcendental meditation, it may be more desirable to lie down flatly and symmetrically on a surface that contours to the shape of your body. As pointed out earlier, the purpose here is to focus inward and to reduce attention to physical requirements like maintaining the prescribed positions for seat, hands, torso, eyes, gaze, face, and legs. Reducing attention to these external physical requirements simply helps to facilitate internalization. Also consider the fact that when experiencing the routine altered states we call sleeping and dreaming, we do so from a lying down position. Though transcendental meditation is profoundly different from sleeping and dreaming, adopting the posture we use when naturally exploring our own internal mindscape may be very helpful in rendering us susceptible to altered states in general.

Breathing

Breathing is central to both meditation and speech. Training yourself to achieve calmness through meditative breathing will translate to achieving calmness through breath while speaking.

Two basic techniques should be employed for meditative breathing:

1. Breathe in through your nose and out through your mouth. In meditation, we want to differentiate inhaling and exhaling as much as possible so we can benefit from the "letting go" effect of breathing out.

2. Breathe deeply, using your **diaphragm** (use your stomach muscles when you breathe), because this assists in the release of natural chemicals that promote relaxation.

Posture and breathing are the cornerstones of good meditative practice, but there are a few additional techniques to share that you might find useful, including vocalization, movement, and guided narration.

Chapter Nine: Relaxing into Your Story: How to use Meditation to Control Speech Anxiety

Meditative Vocalization

Some meditators, especially transcendentalists, like to use single-syllable sounds, words, or even phrases in their meditation practice. This is referred to as chanting or meditative vocalization. Some will even claim that vocalizing brings them into synchronization with the universe. Others use meditative vocalization as a tool to materialize the intention of turning inward.

The best place to begin meditative vocalization is after time, place, posture, and settling have been accomplished, and "letting go" needs to be achieved. For basic mediation practice, it's best to choose a word or sound that is consistent with meditative breathing, which makes use of the diaphragm muscle located in the abdomen. The single syllable term "om," which is preferred by Tibetan Buddhists practicing "presence" meditation, is a good example of a sound that is consistent with meditative breathing. The chant is vocalized upon exhaling and is stretched out to synchronize with the depth and pace of the meditator's breathing pattern.

Turning inward and focusing on transcendence is achieved through imagination of the sound of the meditative vocalization after it has been extensively repeated until the meditator can mentally reproduce every aspect of the sound's quality.

However, the most interesting aspect of meditative vocalization (for our purposes) is the fact that it shares everything in common with the act of speaking. Speeches are, in essence, a complex combination of vocalization patterns that contain semantic meaning. Therefore, it's possible to focus in on a series of key phrases from your presentation and use meditation as a way to practice them individually and make them resonate exactly the way you want them to.

Every good story or presentation should have a number of pithy, important phrases built into it. Look at these as powerful moments that give you a special opportunity to connect with your audience. It's essential to be consciously aware of these opportunities as you construct your speech and then identify these phrases for meditation. Identify and focus on only one phrase per meditation session.

Meditative Movement

Not all meditation needs to occur in a seated posture with crossed legs and hands resting on your thighs. Druidic meditation teacher Nimue Brown (2012) points out that "the prolonged repetition of any movement can encourage a trance state." While this is true in general, not every kind of movement is ideal for entering into a meditative frame of mind. In general terms, repeated movements that are both natural and fluid are best for invoking meditation. Natural movements are comfortable to perform and are consistent with the "affordances" or "implied functions" of your body. For example, walking is an affordance of your legs and grabbing is an affordance of your hands. Fluid movements, on the other hand, are cyclical and make use of momentum when performed. Once again, walking is a good example, but so is rowing a boat, riding a bike, or using a hula-hoop.

If you want to experiment with movement in meditation, you should begin with walking. Move at a natural, fluid pace and stay present with the sensations associated with your physical surroundings. Try to resist the temptation to daydream by focusing on your breathing, the shifting of your weight as you move through space and the feeling of the ground underneath your feet. Once you have a sense of how to enter a meditative state in this way, you can experiment with other natural/fluid movements as well.

It's worthy of note that "fluency" (the ability to speak smoothly without stammering) is a critical factor in effective speech presentation. Fluency of speech and fluidity of movement in meditation share a neurological relationship, so if you practice fluid meditative movement prior to presenting a speech you will enhance your fluency in front of the room.

Guided Narration

A guided narrative meditation or "pathworking" is a form of transcendental meditation which relies upon narration as a means of navigating the inner world of the psyche. Despite the mystical and esoteric connotations of this word and its definition, guided narration can be an effective way for structuring scenarios that unlock your creativity and untapped personal potential, especially with respect to storytelling. After all, guided narration primarily consists of a simple story with a challenge that must be confronted at the end. Vivid descriptions, events, and a climax are just as important here as they are for an effective narrative speech. But to explain guided narration most effectively, we have to understand it as a procedure with a beginning, middle, and end. This brings us to the final section of the chapter: procedure.

PROCEDURE

The basic procedure for guided narration includes settling exercises, the description of sensory details, events leading to a challenge, the challenge itself, and the resolution. However, pathworkings or guided narrations should always be situated within the broader procedure of meditation that was touched upon earlier under the "practice" section and then described in more detail under the "technique" section. This includes choosing a time and space, assuming a meditative posture, settling mind and body, and letting go through the breath.

Chödrön (2013) recommends the procedure of moving through the seven points of meditative posture described earlier to focus or refocus the mind on meditation. Once again, these include: seat, hands, torso, eyes, gaze, face, and legs. For those who don't use a sitting posture or prefer a different method, I recommend proceeding through joint relaxation exercises, beginning with the ankles and proceeding to the knees, hips, spine, shoulders and the base of the skull. Focus in on each joint or set of joints as you inhale, and then release all of the tension from them as you exhale.

Returning to the procedure for guided narration, one should substitute the last step of "letting go through the breath" with the step of entering into the scene of the story. Perhaps a good way to describe this process is "exhaling into the story."

Once you have settled physically and mentally, place your attention on the sensory details associated with the scenario for the purpose of establishing a sense of place through description. When you have achieved this, move forward with events leading to the ultimate challenge you will face. The way you respond to the challenge is where you find the core value of performing this exercise, and it should be completely spontaneous to that moment. The sample below is a very simple guided narration that contains these components:

1. You are standing alone in a forest, surrounded by tall evergreens. The air is dry and the ground is cold. You can feel pine needles strewn beneath your bare feet. There is a slight breeze and light filters brightly through the shadows created by the trees. The smell of pine and a hint of smoke linger in the air, but it's oddly silent until you hear your name spoken faintly in the distance. The voice is so soft that you're not sure if you've imagined it.

2. You follow the voice through the forest. (Add spontaneous sensory experiences.)

3. You come to a clearing at the edge of a lake when you hear the voice again. It sounds oddly familiar to you, but it's coming from across the water on the opposite side of the lake.

4. You swim across the lake. (Add spontaneous sensory experiences.)

5. You crawl out of the water onto a sandy beach that extends for miles in front of you. Once again you hear the voice and you follow it into the distance.

6. You see the faint image of a figure far away. You walk toward the figure. (Add spontaneous sensory experiences.)

7. After what seems like an eternity, you stand before the figure and you realize that the figure is you. Both hands are stretched out in front and they are grasping cloth bags.

8. You choose one of the bags. What is inside? (Add spontaneous sensory experiences.)

The exercise above begins with detailed sensory experiences (the forest) intended to draw the meditator into the scene before guiding them through a series of events (walking through the forest, swimming through the lake, walking on the beach) and, ultimately, a challenge ("choosing one of the bags"). If you are designing your own guided meditation, it's essential not to provide too much detail, so that your own subconscious imagination can manifest through your meditative state and bring to light spontaneous realizations and deep insights. It's also advisable to have someone read the guided narration to you as you meditate or, alternatively, record your voice and play it back as you meditate, because it's not effective to attempt to read and meditate at the same time.

The close connection between guided narration and narrative speech presentation should be readily apparent through the example above, but in case it's not, suffice it to say that any story is a possible object for meditation that will both enhance your knowledge of the story and offer insights into its value system as well as its informative and persuasive potential.

OPTIMAL STATES OF MEDITATION AND PERFORMANCE

Through a commitment to meditation, it is possible to apply the practices, techniques, and procedures of meditation to the public speaking scenario so completely that the act of speaking in public is itself a meditative act. Transcendental meditation may serve as a tool to aid creativity in storytelling and narrative development, while presence meditation provides a means to reduce anxiety and synchronize speaker and audience into a dynamic and emergent flow of ideas. Think of it as a kind of cerebral judo wherein you are channeling different energies from yourself and the audience into an engaging and spontaneous performance of words, voice, movement, and gesture. However, the common element here is flow. You can't fight your way through a speech performance. You have to go with the flow, incorporating overt and subtle feedback cues from the audience on the fly and directing their energy toward the purposes of your message.

The key to experiencing this sense of flow begins with the meditative prerequisite of being present in the moment. Chödrön (2013) observes that "The present moment is the generative fire of our meditation. It is what propels us toward transformation. In other words, the present moment is the fuel for your personal journey." By remaining present in the moment, we stay fluid and, thus, capable of responding and adapting in the moment as conditions emerge. The way to do this initially is through the breath, but as you become more advanced in your practice and study of meditation, you will find that the objects of your meditation become more complex, and though the breath remains essential to both meditation and speech, the speech itself (if practiced correctly) becomes an object of meditation.

REFERENCES

Brown, Nimue (2012). *Druidry and Meditation: Exploring How Meditation Can Enhance Your Druidic Practice.* Moon Books: Alresford, Hants, UK.

Chödrön, Pema (2013). *How to Meditate: A Practical Guide to Making Friends with Your Mind.* Sounds True: Boulder, CO, USA.

Davis, Roy Eugene (1995/2011). *An Easy Guide to Meditation.* The Center for Spiritual Awareness, Lakemont, GA, USA.

Paxson, Diana L. (2008). *Trance-Portation: Learning to Navigate the Inner World.* Weiser Books: San Francisco, CA.

Sheridan, Tai (2011). *Buddha in Blue Jeans: An Extremely Short Simple Zen Guide to Sitting Quietly and Being Buddha.* Kindle: Tai Sheridan.

Appendix A:
Analysis of Folktales

The Girl without Hands

Translated from Kinder- und Hausmärchen
(Grimm, J.L,C & Grimm, W.C., 1857)

A miller had fallen further and further into poverty and had nothing more than his mill and a big apple tree behind it. One day, he had gone into the forest to get wood when an old man walked up to him whom he had never seen before and said, "Why do you torture yourself with woodcutting? I will make you rich, if you promise me what stands behind your mill."

"What else can that be besides my apple tree?" thought the miller. He said "yes," and relinquished it to the strange man.

The old man laughed derisively and said, "After three years, I will come and take what belongs to me," and went away.

When the miller went home, his wife approached him and said, "Tell me, miller, where did all of the riches in our house suddenly come from? All of a sudden, all of the boxes and cabinets are full. No one brought it in and I don't know how it happened."

He answered, "That comes from a strange man, who approached me in the forest and had promised me great riches; for that I have relinquished to him what stands behind the mill: we can surely give the big apple tree for that."

"Oh, husband," said the wife, horrified, "that was the devil. He didn't mean the apple tree, but our daughter, who stands behind the mill and sweeps the yard."

The miller's daughter was a beautiful and pious girl, and lived the three years in fear of God and without sin.

As the time was now at an end, and the day came when the evil one would take her away, she washed herself clean and made a circle around herself with chalk. The devil appeared very early, but he couldn't come near her. Angrily, he said to the miller, "Take all water away from her, so she can wash no more, because otherwise I have no power over her."

The miller was afraid and did it.

On the next morning the devil came again, but she had cried on her hands, and they were completely clean. Once again he couldn't approach her and said furiously to the miller, "Cut her hands off, otherwise I cannot harm her."

The miller was horrified and answered, "How could I cut off the hands of my own child?"

Then the devil threatened him and said, "If you don't do it, you are mine, and I will take you yourself."

The father was afraid, and he promised to obey him. Then he went to the girl and said, "My child, if I don't cut off both your hands, the devil will lead me away, and out of fear I promised it. But help me with my need and forgive me for what evil I do to you."

She answered, "Dear father, do with me what you will, I am your child."

Thereupon she laid down both hands and let them be cut off.

The devil came for the third time, but she had cried so long and so much on her stumps, that they were completely clean. Then he had to give up and lost all right to her.

The miller said to her, "I have won so much good through you, that I will keep you in luxury for your whole life."

But she answered, "I can't stay here; I will go away. Sympathetic people will give me just as much as I need."

Thereupon she had her mutilated arms bound to her back, and with the sunrise she went on her way and went the whole day until it was night. Then she came to a royal garden, and by moonlight she saw that there were trees with beautiful fruits inside; but she couldn't get in because there was water surrounding it. And because she had walked the whole day and hadn't enjoyed a bite, and hunger tortured her, she thought, "Oh, if only I were in there, so that I could eat some of that fruit, otherwise I must languish."

Then she fell to her knees, called to God the father and prayed. At once an angel came, who made a lock in the water, so that the ditch was dry and she could go through. Now she went in the garden and the angel went with her. She saw a tree with fruit; they were beautiful pears, but they were all counted. Then she walked over and ate one from the tree with her mouth to quiet her hunger, but no more. The gardener saw this, but because the angel stood by, he was afraid and thought the girl was a ghost, so he silenced himself and didn't trust to call or speak to the ghost. As she had eaten the pear, she was satisfied and went and hid herself in the bush.

The king, to whom the gardener belonged, came down the next day. He counted and saw that one of the pears was missing, and asked the gardener where it would have gone: it didn't lie under the tree and was just gone. The gardener answered, "The previous night, a ghost came in here that had no hands and ate one down with its mouth."

The king said, "How did the ghost come in here over the water? And where did it go after he had eaten the pear?"

The gardener answered, "Someone came in snow-white clothing from heaven, who had closed the locks and held back the water, so that the ghost could go through the ditch. And since it had to be an angel, I was afraid; I didn't ask and I didn't call out. After the ghost had eaten the pear, it went back again."

The king said, "If what you say holds up, I will stand guard with you tonight."

As it was dark, the king came into the garden and brought a priest with him who was to talk to the ghost. All three sat themselves under the tree and paid attention. At midnight the girl came crawling out of the bush, walked to the tree, and again ate a pear from the tree with her mouth; next to her, though, stood the angel in the white dress.

Then the priest went forward and said, "Have you come from God or from the world? Are you a ghost or a person?"

She answered, "I am not a ghost, rather a poor person, abandoned by all except God."

The king said, "If you're abandoned by the whole world, then I won't abandon you."

He took her with him into his royal castle and because she was so beautiful and pious, he loved her from the heart, had silver hands made for her and took her as his wife.

After a year the king had to travel afield, and he commended the young queen to his mother and said, "When she is ready to give birth, keep her well and care for her and write me a letter immediately."

So she gave birth to a beautiful son. The old mother wrote in a hurry and reported to him the happy news. But the messenger rested along the way at a stream, and because he was tired from the long journey, he fell asleep. Then the devil came, who was always trying to bring the pious queen to harm, and exchanged the letter for another, wherein was written that the queen had brought a changeling into the world.

As the king read the letter he was horrified and was saddened, but he wrote an answer: his mother should keep the queen well and care for her until his arrival. The messenger went back with the letter, rested himself in the same exact place and fell asleep again. Then the devil came again and put another letter in his pocket upon which was written that the king's mother should kill the queen with her child.

The old mother was so terribly horrified when she received the letter that she couldn't believe it and wrote the king again, but she received no other answer because the devil planted a false letter on the messenger each time, and in the last letter it was written that she should also keep the queen's tongue and eyes for proof.

But the old mother cried that such innocent blood should be spilled, so she had a deer brought to her in the night, cut out its tongue and eyes, and kept them. Then she said to the queen, "I cannot have you killed, as the king orders, but you cannot stay here any longer: go with your child into the world and never come back." She tied her child to her back and the poor woman went away with tears in her eyes.

She arrived in a big wild forest, where she knelt and prayed to God, and the angel of the Lord appeared to her and led her to a small house upon which was a sign with the words "everyone lives free here." A snow-white virgin came out of the little house and who said, "Welcome Lady Queen," and led her inside. Then she untied the small boy from her back and held him to her breast so that he drank and then laid him on a beautifully made bed.

The poor woman asked, "How did you know that I was a queen?"

The white virgin answered, "I am an angel, sent from God, to care for you and your child."

She stayed there in the house seven years and was well cared for, and through God's mercy, and due to her piousness, her severed hands grew back.

The king finally returned home from afield, and his first priority was that he would see his wife and child. The old mother began to cry and said, "You evil man, what have you written to me, that I should end the life of two innocent souls," and showed him the two letters that the evil one had falsified and said further, "I did as you have ordered," and showed him the proof, tongue and eyes .

Then the king started to cry so bitterly over his poor wife and his little son that the old mother had pity and she said to him "Have peace, they still live. I had a doe slaughtered secretly and took the proof from it, but I tied the child to your wife's back and told her to go into the world, and she had to promise never again to come back here because you were so furious with her."

With this, the king said, "I will go as far as the sky is blue, and not eat or drink until I have found my dear wife and my child again, if they haven't been killed or died of hunger in that time." Thereupon the king traveled about for seven years and searched for them in all the rocky cliffs and caves, but he didn't find them and thought they had starved. He didn't eat or drink during this whole time, but God preserved him.

Finally he came into a big forest and found the small house inside, whereupon the sign was with the words, "everyone lives free here." The white virgin came out, took him by the hand, led him inside, and said, "Be welcome Lord King," and asked him where he came from.

He answered, "I have been traveling around for nearly seven years and seek my wife with her child, but I can't find her."

The angel offered him food and drink, but he didn't take it, and wanted only to rest a little. Then he laid himself to sleep and covered his face with a cloth. Upon that, the angel went into the chamber where the queen sat with her child, that she appropriately named Agony and said to her, "Go out together with your child, your husband has come."

She went over to where he lay and the cloth fell from his visage. Then she said, "Agony, pick up your father's cloth and cover his face again."

The child lifted it up and covered his face with it again. The king heard that in his light sleep and gladly let the cloth fall again. The little boy was innocent, though, and said, "Dear mother, how can I cover my father's face, I have no father in the world. I have learned the prayer, our father who art in heaven. You have said my father would be in heaven and would be God Almighty. How can I acknowledge such a wild man? He is not my father."

As the king heard that he sat up and asked who she was. Then she said, "I am your wife and that is your son, Agony."

And he saw her living hands and said, "My wife had silver hands."

She answered, "Merciful God let my natural hands grow back again," and the angel went in the chamber, took the silver hands and showed them to him.

Then he saw with certainty for the first time that it was his dear wife and dear child, and kissed her and was happy, and said "A heavy stone has fallen from my heart."

Then the angel of God fed them together again, and then they went home to his old mother. There was great happiness everywhere and the king and queen had another wedding, and they lived pleasantly until their blessed end.

Breakdown of Narrative Components in "The Girl without Hands"

Background 1	A miller had fallen further and further into poverty and had nothing more than his mill and a big apple tree behind it.
Event 1	One day, he had gone into the forest to get wood when an old man walked up to him whom he had never seen before and said, "Why do you torture yourself with woodcutting? I will make you rich, if you promise me what stands behind your mill." "What else can that be besides my apple tree?" thought the miller. He said "yes," and relinquished it to the strange man. The old man laughed derisively and said, "After three years, I will come and take what belongs to me," and went away.
Event 2	When the miller went home, his wife approached him and said, "Tell me, miller, where did all of the riches in our house suddenly come from? All of a sudden, all of the boxes and cabinets are full. No one brought it in and I don't know how it happened." He answered, "That comes from a strange man, who approached me in the forest and had promised me great riches; for that I have relinquished to him what stands behind the mill: we can surely give the big apple tree for that." "Oh, husband," said the wife, horrified, "that was the devil. He didn't mean the apple tree, but our daughter, who stands behind the mill and sweeps the yard."
Transition/ Background 2	The miller's daughter was a beautiful and pious girl, and lived the three years in fear of God and without sin.
Event 3	As the time was now at an end, and the day came when the evil one would take her away, she washed herself clean and made a circle around herself with chalk. The devil appeared very early, but he couldn't come near her. Angrily, he said to the miller, "Take all water away from her, so she can wash no more, because otherwise I have no power over her." The miller was afraid and did it.
Event 4	On the next morning the devil came again, but she had cried on her hands, and they were completely clean. Once again he couldn't approach her and said furiously to the miller, "Cut her hands off, otherwise I cannot harm her." The miller was horrified and answered, "How could I cut off the hands of my own child?" Then the devil threatened him and said, "If you don't do it, you are mine, and I will take you yourself." The father was afraid, and he promised to obey him.
Event 5	Then he went to the girl and said, "My child, if I don't cut off both your hands, the devil will lead me away, and out of fear I promised it. But help me with my need and forgive me for what evil I do to you." She answered, "Dear father, do with me what you will, I am your child." Thereupon she laid down both hands and let them be cut off.
Event 6	The devil came for the third time, but she had cried so long and so much on her stumps, that they were completely clean. Then he had to give up and lost all right to her. The miller said to her, "I have won so much good through you, that I will keep you in luxury for your whole life." But she answered, "I can't stay here; I will go away. Sympathetic people will give me just as much as I need."

Appendix A: Analysis of Folktales

Breakdown of Narrative Components in "The Girl without Hands"

Transition/ Background 3	Thereupon she had her mutilated arms bound to her back, and with the sunrise she went on her way and went the whole day until it was night.
Event 7	Then she came to a royal garden, and by moonlight she saw that there were trees with beautiful fruits inside; but she couldn't get in because there was water surrounding it. And because she had walked the whole day and hadn't enjoyed a bite, and hunger tortured her, she thought, "Oh, if only I were in there, so that I could eat some of that fruit, otherwise I must languish." Then she fell to her knees, called to God the father and prayed. At once an angel came, who made a lock in the water, so that the ditch was dry and she could go through. Now she went in the garden and the angel went with her. She saw a tree with fruit; they were beautiful pears, but they were all counted. Then she walked over and ate one from the tree with her mouth to quiet her hunger, but no more. The gardener saw this, but because the angel stood by, he was afraid and thought the girl was a ghost, so he silenced himself and didn't trust to call or speak to the ghost. As she had eaten the pear, she was satisfied and went and hid herself in the bush.
Event 8	The king, to whom the gardener belonged, came down the next day. He counted and saw that one of the pears was missing, and asked the gardener where it would have gone: it didn't lie under the tree and was just gone. The gardener answered, "The previous night, a ghost came in here that had no hands and ate one down with its mouth." The king said, "How did the ghost come in here over the water? And where did it go after he had eaten the pear?" The gardener answered, "Someone came in snow-white clothing from heaven, who had closed the locks and held back the water, so that the ghost could go through the ditch. And since it had to be an angel, I was afraid; I didn't ask and I didn't call out. After the ghost had eaten the pear, it went back again." The king said, "If what you say holds up, I will stand guard with you tonight."
Event 9	As it was dark, the king came into the garden and brought a priest with him who was to talk to the ghost. All three sat themselves under the tree and paid attention. At midnight the girl came crawling out of the bush, walked to the tree, and again ate a pear from the tree with her mouth; next to her, though, stood the angel in the white dress. Then the priest went forward and said, "Have you come from God or from the world? Are you a ghost or a person?" She answered, "I am not a ghost, rather a poor person, abandoned by all except God." The king said, "If you're abandoned by the whole world, then I won't abandon you."
Transition/ Background 4	He took her with him into his royal castle and because she was so beautiful and pious, he loved her from the heart, had silver hands made for her and took her as his wife.
Event 10	After a year the king had to travel afield, and he commended the young queen to his mother and said, "When she is ready to give birth, keep her well and care for her and write me a letter immediately."
Event 11	So she gave birth to a beautiful son.

	Breakdown of Narrative Components in "The Girl without Hands"
Event 13	But the messenger rested along the way at a stream, and because he was tired from the long journey, he fell asleep. Then the devil came, who was always trying to bring the pious queen to harm, and exchanged the letter for another, wherein was written that the queen had brought a changeling into the world.
Event 14	As the king read the letter he was horrified and was saddened, but he wrote an answer: his mother should keep the queen well and care for her until his arrival.
Event 15	The messenger went back with the letter, rested himself in the same exact place and fell asleep again. Then the devil came again and put another letter in his pocket upon which was written that the king's mother should kill the queen with her child.
Transition/ Background 5	The old mother was so terribly horrified when she received the letter that she couldn't believe it and wrote the king again, but she received no other answer because the devil planted a false letter on the messenger each time, and in the last letter it was written that she should also keep the queen's tongue and eyes for proof.
Event 16	But the old mother cried that such innocent blood should be spilled, so she had a deer brought to her in the night, cut out its tongue and eyes, and kept them.
Event 17	Then she said to the queen, "I cannot have you killed, as the king orders, but you cannot stay here any longer: go with your child into the world and never come back." She tied her child to her back and the poor woman went away with tears in her eyes.
Event 18	She arrived in a big wild forest, where she knelt and prayed to God, and the angel of the Lord appeared to her and led her to a small house upon which was a sign with the words "everyone lives free here." A snow white virgin came out of the little house and who said, "Welcome Lady Queen," and led her inside. Then she untied the small boy from her back and held him to her breast so that he drank and then laid him on a beautifully made bed. The poor woman asked, "How did you know that I was a queen?" The white virgin answered, "I am an angel, sent from God, to care for you and your child."
Transition/ Background 6	She stayed there in the house seven years and was well cared for, and through God's mercy, and due to her piousness, her severed hands grew back.
Event 19	The king finally returned home from afield, and his first priority was that he would see his wife and child. The old mother began to cry and said, "You evil man, what have you written to me, that I should end the life of two innocent souls," and showed him the two letters that the evil one had falsified and said further, "I did as you have ordered," and showed him the proof, tongue and eyes. Then the king started to cry so bitterly over his poor wife and his little son that the old mother had pity and she said to him "Have peace, they still live. I had a doe slaughtered secretly and took the proof from it, but I tied the child to your wife's back and told her to go into the world, and she had to promise never again to come back here because you were so furious with her." With this, the king said, "I will go as far as the sky is blue, and not eat or drink until I have found my dear wife and my child again, if they haven't been killed or died of hunger in that time."
Transition/ Background 7	Thereupon the king traveled about for seven years and searched for them in all the rocky cliffs and caves, but he didn't find them and thought they had starved. He didn't eat or drink during this whole time, but God preserved him.

Appendix A: Analysis of Folktales

Breakdown of Narrative Components in "The Girl without Hands"

Event 20 (Climax)	Finally he came into a big forest and found the small house inside, whereupon the sign was with the words, "everyone lives free here." The white virgin came out, took him by the hand, led him inside, and said, "Be welcome Lord King," and asked him where he came from. He answered, "I have been traveling around for nearly seven years and seek my wife with her child, but I can't find her." The angel offered him food and drink, but he didn't take it, and wanted only to rest a little. Then he laid himself to sleep and covered his face with a cloth. Upon that, the angel went into the chamber where the queen sat with her child, that she appropriately named Agony and said to her, "Go out together with your child, your husband has come." She went over to where he lay and the cloth fell from his visage. Then she said, "Agony, pick up your father's cloth and cover his face again." The child lifted it up and covered his face with it again. The king heard that in his light sleep and gladly let the cloth fall again. The little boy was innocent, though, and said, "Dear mother, how can I cover my father's face, I have no father in the world. I have learned the prayer, our father who art in heaven. You have said my father would be in heaven and would be God Almighty. How can I acknowledge such a wild man? He is not my father." As the king heard that he sat up and asked who she was. Then she said, "I am your wife and that is your son, Agony." And he saw her living hands and said, "My wife had silver hands." She answered, "Merciful God let my natural hands grow back again," and the angel went in the chamber, took the silver hands and showed them to him. Then he saw with certainty for the first time that it was his dear wife and dear child, and kissed her and was happy, and said "A heavy stone has fallen from my heart." Then the angel of God fed them together again, and then they went home to his old mother.
Background 8	There was great happiness everywhere and the king and queen had another wedding, and they lived pleasantly until their blessed end.

Appendix A: Analysis of Folktales

EXPLANATION OF NARRATIVE COMPONENTS

- Background 1: Establishes the initial conflict.
- Event 1: The miller makes a deal with the devil.
- Event 2: The miller discovers his daughter was standing behind the mill.
- Transition/Background 2: This serves to establish the character of the miller's daughter and to indicate the passage of three years.
- Event 3: The devil attempts to take the miller's daughter, but she had washed her hands.
- Event 4: The devil attempts to take the miller's daughter again, but she had cried on her hands.
- Event 5: The miller cuts his daughter's hands off.
- Event 6: The devil attempts to take the miller's daughter for a third time, but she had cried on the stumps of her hand.
- Transition/Background 3: Time elapses as the miller's daughter wanders far from home.
- Event 7: The miller's daughter arrives at the king's garden and, with the help of an angel, she crosses the water and eats a pear.
- Event 8: The king discovers that one of his pears is missing and decides to keep watch with the gardener the next evening.
- Event 9: The king comes with a priest the next evening, and when the miller's daughter appears, the priest speaks to her.
- Transition/Background 4: This describes several events transpiring over a nondescript period of time: the king takes the miller's daughter into his castle, he has silver hands made for her and he takes her as his wife.
- Event 10: The king goes afield and tells his mother to watch after his wife as she is to give birth.
- Event 11: The queen (miller's daughter) gives birth.
- Event 12: The king's mother writes to him of the happy news.

- Event 13: The messenger stops along the way and the devil swaps the note for one that says the child is a changeling.
- Event 14: The king is horrified by the news, but writes back that she should care for the queen until he gets back.
- Event 15: The messenger rests in the same spot and the devil swaps the note again for one saying she should kill the queen.
- Transition/Background 5: This indicates several messages were sent back and forth until the king demands proof of the queen's death in the form of her carved out eyes and tongue.
- Event 16: The king's mother has a doe slaughtered to provide evidence for the king.
- Event 17: The king's mother sends the queen on her way and tells her not to return.
- Event 18: The queen arrives with her child at a little house in the forest where she's cared for by a snow-white virgin.
- Transition/Background 6: This indicates that time elapses and the queen's hands grow back.
- Event 19: The king returns home and learns of what happened. He vows to go out and find his wife and child.
- Transition/Background 7: Time elapses as the king searches for seven years.
- Event 20: The king arrives at the small house in the woods and finds his wife and son. They return home.
- Background 8: They lived happily ever after.

Appendix B: Analysis of The Moth

A Very Dangerous Person

URL http://themoth.org/posts/stories/a-very-dangerous-person

Outline

- Central Idea: "Crisis greatly contributes to the development of identity.
- Event 1: December 25, 1960. Paul becomes labeled a "dangerous person."
  - »» Italian Christmas dinner in the south side of Chicago, 1960.
  - »» Paul and his cousin Rico are jumping off the couch.
  - »» Paul topples a bottle of wine and his Uncle Mike, a cop, handcuffs him to the radiator.
  - »» After begging for a while, Uncle Mike uncuffs him, but Paul hits him in the head with a bottle of wine and goes after Uncle Mike's gun.
  - »» At that moment, Paul became labeled "a dangerous person."
- Transition: "For the next twelve years, I did things that probably weren't too good."
- Event 2: January 8, 1973.
  - »» I'm standing on the Dan Ryan Expressway with my thumb out underneath the "Magic Kiss" sign, hitchhiking to go back to Galesburg to finish my last semester of college.
  - »» Cars pass.
  - »» An Olds 88 stops and picks me up.

- »» Inside, the car is a mess and it stinks.
- »» Paul talks to the driver. He reminds him of his brother-in-law's father, Wally.
- »» He notices a clown nose and a red wig.
- »» The driver says to Paul, "If you let me play with your d***, I'll drive you to Galesburg."
- »» Paul refuses, but the driver persists.
- »» A pistol falls onto the floorboard.
- »» Paul thinks back to that Christmas with Uncle Mike and he says, "You have picked up a very dangerous person. I will grab the f****** steering wheel of this car and I will kill both of us. Let me out."
- Event 3: December 22, 1978.
  - »» Paul's at his sister's house on a Friday night.
  - »» John Drury comes on the news and he says, "A grisly discovery has been made at Norwood Park."
  - »» Paul's sister comes out and says, "That looks like your father, Wally."
- Event 4: May 10, 1994.
  - »» "John Wayne Gacy was executed for killing 33 young men. Because of my Uncle Mike and my crisis with my identity, I was fortunate not to be number 34."

Appendix B: Analysis of The Moth

Exercise: Answer the following questions.

1. Provide a value statement for this story.

2. What's effective about the choice of events and how they're organized?

3. What's effective about the speaker's delivery? Focus on paralanguage and chronemics.

Appendix C: Analysis of TED.com

Informative TED Talks

Speech Title: "The Clues to a Great Story"
Speaker: Andrew Stanton
URL: http://www.ted.com/talks/andrew_stanton_the_clues_to_a_great_story
General Purpose: To inform
Specific Purpose: To teach the audience the techniques of good storytelling

Reverse Outline

- Introduction

    - »» Attention: The story about the bar in Scotland.

    - »» Central Idea: There are underlying principles that apply to storytelling.

    - »» Importance: Stories are a key part of our personal identity.

    - »» Credibility: Also see the story about the bar in Scotland.

    - »» Preview: Stanton tells us he's going to use a timeline of important moments in his life to structure the speech; however, these are not his main points, just the structure he will use to present his main points. The actual main points of the speech are features that good stories have in common.

- Body

    - »» Main Point 1: Make me care.

        - »The example of channel surfing.

    - »» Main Point 2: Make a promise.

        - »John Carter (2012) movie clip.

        - »The slingshot metaphor.

»» Main Point 3: The "unifying theory of 2 + 2"

»"We're compelled to deduce and to deduct, because that's what we do in real-life. It's this well-organized absence of information that draws us in."

»The infant/puppy metaphor.

»WALL-E (2008) movie clip.

»"Make the audience put things together."

»» Main Point 4: Stories should be inevitable but not predictable.

»There is no single formula for good storytelling.

»» Main Point 5: Characters should have a spine.

»Michael Corleone: "please his father"

»WALL-E: "find the beauty"

»Marlin: "prevent harm"

»Woody: "do what is best for his child"

»» Main Point 6: Change is fundamental to storytelling.

»"If things go static, stories die, because life is never static."

»Quote from William Archer: "Drama is anticipation mingled with uncertainty."

»» Main Point 7: Storytelling has guidelines, not hard/fast rules

»No songs

»No "I want" moment

»No happy village

»No love story

»No villain

»» Main Point 8: You have to like your main character.

»Toy Story (1995) movie clip.

- »» Main Point 9: Stories should have a strong theme.
    - »Lawrence of Arabia (1962) movie clip.
    - »"Who are you?"
    - »"A strong theme is always running through a well-told story."
- »» Main Point 10: Stories should instill a sense of wonder.
    - »Bambi (1942) movie clip.
- »» Main Point 11: Use what you know to tell a story.
    - »Andrew shares his story of his being born premature and almost dying and how this has affected his life.
    - »Finding Nemo (2003) movie clip.
- Conclusion
- »» Recap of Main Points: There is no recap of main points.
- »» Restatement of the Central Idea: The central idea is not restated.
- »» Conclusive Statement: And that's what ultimately led me to speaking to you here at TEDTalk today.

CONTENT CRITIQUE

The strength of this speech rests in its structure and use of examples to support the main points. Stanton starts off with an off-color joke that takes the form of a short story about an old man in a bar. This joke serves three purposes in the context of his presentation:

1. To gain the audience's attention. Stanton could have told any number of jokes or stories, but it seems likely he selected this one to surprise the audience a little bit and grab hold of their attention.
2. To gain credibility. Because the purpose of Stanton's speech is to teach storytelling, it is appropriate that he is able to demonstrate his ability to tell a good story. To be sure, his reputation as a film director and writer precede

him, but there's nothing like an immediate demonstration of skill to impress an audience.

3. To introduce his central idea. The most obvious purpose of this story is to serve as a lead-in to the metaphor of storytelling as joke telling, which appears to be the central idea of this speech. Stanton doesn't elaborate very much, but he clearly makes a comparison between jokes and stories based on the role of anticipation.

Stanton establishes the structure of his speech at the end of the introduction when he explains that he will present a timeline going backwards, explaining the important lessons about storytelling that he's learned in his own life. Doing this allows him to move from more specific, technical ideas like the "unifying theory of 2+2" to more basic story values such as "wonder." It also creates a strong connection between him and his audience since he's asking them to go on a journey back in time with him through his own life and experience. Stanton's main points are nested within these experiences that are roughly arranged based on date beginning with the present moment in 2012 and going all the way back to his birth as a premature baby.

Notice also how each of Stanton's main points are very clearly stated and supported with examples. For instance, he shows numerous specific film clips and explains how they demonstrate the point he is making. Simply showing a photograph or a clip of video does little to teach an audience, it's in the explanation provided between the video and the main point that understanding occurs. To illustrate this point, watch the scene from WALL-E (2008) carefully. Stanton introduces the "unifying theory of 2+2" and then explains it by referencing how the film requires the audience to interpret the emotions of the characters on screen.

At the end of the speech, Stanton returns to his own personal story about being born premature and feeling the pressure to make something out of the second chance he was given. Once again, this creates a strong connection with the audience at the same time that it demonstrates the point he's making (use what you know to tell a story), and demonstrates very well that he's capable of telling a good story.

DELIVERY CRITIQUE

Andrew Stanton makes use of all the techniques of good delivery, including posture, gesture, facial expressions, eye contact, paralanguage, chronemics, and proxemics. However, not every technique is equally well utilized. Notice how he often glances down between ideas during his presentation. He does this because there is a screen located at the edge of the stage providing him with an outline of his talk. Relying on this too heavily reduces the connection to the audience that only eye contact can provide and also (at times) disrupts the pacing of his speech because he requires a second to read his notes on stage. The collective effect here is very subtle and the impact of these small mistakes is almost imperceptible to an uncritical audience. Furthermore, we must remember that Stanton is a filmmaker and not a professional speaker, though he does present his ideas well overall. He also has the advantage of a prestigious artistic reputation behind him. An unknown speaker would likely be judged more explicitly on delivery performance since the audience has much less to base their assessment on.

NARRATIVE TOOLS

Stanton uses short stories in this speech, but this is not the only narrative tool present here. Notice how his organization of the speech through reverse chronology provides a narrative structure moving back in time based on his own experiences of learning how to tell stories. This certainly provides a personal connection with the audience (establishing what Aristotle would call his "ethos"), but the main purpose of this structure is to provide a context for the presentation of the main points he's going to share with us about good storytelling. By going backwards, he also creates the effect of moving deeper and deeper into the psychology of narrative, beginning with more obvious concrete points like "make me care" and "make a promise" to psychic abstractions such as the notion of "wonder."

Ultimately, there is a real sense of integrity in this speech because Stanton employs the same tools that he's teaching to accomplish his specific purpose.

Speech Title: "Your Body Language Shapes Who You Are"
Speaker: Amy Cuddy
URL: https://www.ted.com/talks/amy_cuddy_your_body_language_shapes_who_you_are/transcript
General Purpose: To inform
Specific Purpose: To inform the audience about power poses, and the consequences of body posture and nonverbal communication.

Reverse Outline

- Introduction
  - »» Attention: Speaker involves the audience in an exercise to introduce the real consequences of nonverbal communication.
    - »"So I want to start by offering you a free no-tech life hack, and all it requires of you is this: that you change your posture for two minutes. But before I give it away, I want to ask you to right now do a little audit of your body and what you're doing with your body. So how many of you are sort of making yourselves smaller? Maybe you're hunching, crossing your legs, maybe wrapping your ankles. Sometimes we hold onto our arms like this. Sometimes we spread out. I see you."
  - »» Central Idea: Body language is a unique code that can change your life.
    - »"So obviously when we think about nonverbal behavior, or body language—but we call it nonverbals as social scientists—it's language, so we think about communication. When we think about communication, we think about interactions. So what is your body language communicating to me? What's mine communicating to you?"
  - »» Importance: Nonverbal communication is powerful and audiences make judgments about you based on your body language.
    - »"I'm hoping that if you learn to tweak this a little bit, it could significantly change the way your life unfolds. And we make sweeping judgments and inferences from body language. And those judgments can predict really meaningful life outcomes like who we hire or promote, who we ask out on a date."

- »» Credibility: The speaker has academic expertise.
    - »"I'm a social psychologist. I study prejudice, and I teach at a competitive business school, so it was inevitable that I would become interested in power dynamics. I became especially interested in nonverbal expressions of power and dominance."
- »» Preview: No preview is given.
- Transition 1
    - »» "And what are nonverbal expressions of power and dominance? Well, this is what they are."
- Body
    - »» Elaboration of Main Point 1: Proxemics involves using the space around you to communicate with others.
        - »"So in the animal kingdom, they are about expanding. So you make yourself big, you stretch out, you take up space, and you're basically opening up."
    - »Supporting Evidence: Speaker provides research into power dynamics and body language.
        - *"She shows that people who are born with sight and people who are congenitally blind do this when they win at a physical competition. So when they cross the finish line and they've won, it doesn't matter if they've never seen anyone do it. They do this. So the arm up in the V, the chin is slightly lifted."
    - »» Elaboration of Main Point 2: Our power is derived from our nonverbal body language.
        - »"What do we do when we feel powerless? We do exactly the opposite. We close up. We wrap ourselves up. We make ourselves small. We don't want to bump into the person next to us. So again, both animals and humans do the same thing."
    - »Supporting Evidence: Speaker has first-hand experience observing students and classroom power dynamics and use of body language.

Appendix C: Analysis of TED.com

- »"So I'm watching this behavior in the classroom, and what do I notice? I notice that MBA students really exhibit the full range of power nonverbals. So you have people who are like caricatures of alphas, really coming into the room, they get right into the middle of the room before class even starts, like they really want to occupy space. When they sit down, they're sort of spread out. They raise their hands like this. You have other people who are virtually collapsing when they come in."

- »» Elaboration of Main Point 3: There is an imbalance of power and participation among women and men in interpersonal communication.

    - »"It seems to be related to gender. So women are much more likely to do this kind of thing than men. Women feel chronically less powerful than men, so this is not surprising. But the other thing I noticed is that it also seemed to be related to the extent to which the students were participating, and how well they were participating."

    - »Supporting Evidence: Body language and participation affect each other and can lead an individual to succeed or fail in college.

    - »"And this is really important in the MBA classroom, because participation counts for half the grade. So business schools have been struggling with this gender grade gap. You get these equally qualified women and men coming in and then you get these differences in grades, and it seems to be partly attributable to participation."

- Elaboration of Main Point 4: Our body language influences our intrapersonal communication and self-esteem.

    - »» "But our question really was, do our nonverbals govern how we think and feel about ourselves?"

    - »» Supporting Evidence: "So, for example, we smile when we feel happy, but also, when we're forced to smile by holding a pen in our teeth like this, it makes us feel happy. So it goes both ways. When it comes to power, it also goes both ways. So when you feel powerful, you're more likely to do this, but it's also possible that when you pretend to be powerful, you are more likely to actually feel powerful."

- Elaboration of Main Point 5: There is a relationship between nonverbal communication and human physiology.

»» "Is it also true that our bodies change our minds?"

»» Supporting Evidence:

»"Physiologically, there also are differences on two key hormones: testosterone, which is the dominance hormone, and cortisol, which is the stress hormone. So what we find is that high-power alpha males in primate hierarchies have high testosterone and low cortisol, and powerful and effective leaders also have high testosterone and low cortisol."

»» Supporting Evidence:

»"So this is what we did. We decided to bring people into the lab and run a little experiment, and these people adopted, for two minutes, either high-power poses or low-power poses, and I'm just going to show you five of the poses, although they took on only two."

»"So this is what happens. They come in, they spit into a vial, we for two minutes say, "You need to do this or this." They don't look at pictures of the poses. We don't want to prime them with a concept of power. We want them to be feeling power, right? So two minutes they do this. We then ask them, "How powerful do you feel?" on a series of items, and then we give them an opportunity to gamble, and then we take another saliva sample. That's it. That's the whole experiment."

- Elaboration of Main Point 6: There are practical aspects of power posing that can help you achieve success.

    »» "But the next question, of course, is can power posing for a few minutes really change your life in meaningful ways?"

    »» (Second Experiment shows the uses of power posing.)

    »» "So we bring people into a lab, and they do either high- or low-power poses again, they go through a very stressful job interview. It's five minutes long. They are being recorded. They're being judged also, and the judges are trained to give no nonverbal feedback, so they look like this."

- Transition 2: Preview of personal narrative.

    »» "So when I tell people about this, that our bodies change our minds and our minds can change our behavior, and our behavior can change our outcomes, they say to me, 'I don't—It feels fake.' Right? So I said, fake it till you make it. I don't—It's not me. I don't want to get there and then still feel like a fraud. I don't want to feel like an impostor. I don't want to get there only to feel like I'm not supposed to be here. And that really resonated with me, because I want to tell you a little story about being an impostor and feeling like I'm not supposed to be here."

- Personal story provided to show how speaker sees the effect of body language on an individual's power dynamics.

    »» "When I was 19, I was in a really bad car accident. I was thrown out of a car, rolled several times. I was thrown from the car. And I woke up in a head injury rehab ward, and I had been withdrawn from college, and I learned that my IQ had dropped by two standard deviations, which was very traumatic."

- Transition to Conclusion: "The last thing I'm going to leave you with is this."
- Conclusion

    »Recap of Main Points: Summary of experimental results.

    »"Tiny tweaks can lead to big changes."

    »"Before you go into the next stressful evaluative situation, for two minutes, try doing this, in the elevator, in a bathroom stall, at your desk behind closed doors. That's what you want to do. Configure your brain to cope the best in that situation. Get your testosterone up. Get your cortisol down."

    »Restatement of the Central Idea: There is no restatement of the centralidea.

    »Conclusive Statement

        *"So I want to ask you first, you know, both to try power posing, and also I want to ask you to share the science, because this is simple. I don't have ego involved in this. (Laughter) Give it away. Share it with people, because the people who can use it the most are the ones with no resources and no technology and no status and no power. Give it to them because they can do it in private. They need their bodies, privacy and two minutes, and

CONTENT CRITIQUE

In this presentation, Amy Cuddy has a clear central idea, and an organized introduction. It should be noted that she uses the word "You" or "Your" fourteen times in the attention getter which is only thirty-five seconds long, and she then asks the audience to audit their current body language. This technique is extremely effective in getting the audience involved with the content of the speech.

Once she's engaged the audience, she proceeds to use "we" to start a discussion on why we need to have a better understanding of the topic. Audiences want to be involved in your speech and this communal approach in the introduction is effective. Amy Cuddy lays out the central idea and the importance of the topic clearly. She then delivers her personal and academic credibility statement with the use of "I," which answers the question to the audience, "Why are you a credible speaker, and why should we listen to you?" The use of visuals in her PowerPoint along with video clips of President Obama and Prime Minster Gordon Brown are effective in getting the audience to see the real consequences of nonverbal communication.

The first three main points and supporting evidence educate the audience on nonverbal communication. By starting with visual examples from the animal kingdom, and proceeding through student classroom participation, Cuddy illustrates how body language is linked to power dynamics.

The fourth to the sixth main points and supporting evidence focus on the use of existing social science research on body language and facial expressions. These main points also include the new experiments that were conducted by Amy Cuddy to see the effect of body language in different settings and scenarios. This area is the most informative for the audience because it is primary-source research and the audience begins to realize how body language and power poses can change their lives.

The conclusive statement is well thought out and asks the audience to take what they learned today and share it with others to improve their lives.

DELIVERY CRITIQUE

We would expect someone presenting on the power of body language to have excellent control over their own body language, and Amy Cuddy excels in this area of speech delivery. She has great visuals, a fluid use of PowerPoint slides, and a video clip to start that are all excellent examples of how to use visuals to enhance your speech. The only weak areas in nonverbal communication that are noticeable are her persistent lip licking and mouth touching. These distracting gestures may be due to initial nervousness, but they improve as the speech progresses.

However, there are some problems in her verbal communication. You can witness her communication apprehension in the rate of her speech, heavy inhaling and breathing at the end of sentences, and a plethora of filler words. Filler words are meaningless words that are added at the end of a sentence, as a vocalized pause to buy time before a next thought is delivered. For example, "umms," "ahhs," "likes," and "you knows."

NARRATIVE TOOLS:

The speaker uses a few techniques of narrative structure in this speech.

First, she chooses you, we, and I as the introduction word choices, which are chronological, and a technique to draw the audience into the speech. We also follow chronologically from the (past) primates to (current) human research on body posture.

Secondly, she uses brief illustrations of student classroom participation and their low- and high-power poses.

Lastly, the most important area that is borrowed from the narrative tradition is the extended personal narrative Cuddy provides that illustrates the central idea of the speech. At the start of the story, her communication apprehension decreases and she uses fewer filler words. Her story of nonverbal communication and the fear of speaking are clearly demonstrated in the story of her academic struggles. It's this narrative that relates the speaker to the audience and informs them that if she could "fake it till she makes it," the audience can surely "fake it till they become it," if they use power poses in their daily interactions.

Appendix C: Analysis of TED.com

SPEECH TITLE: "8 Secrets of Success"
SPEAKER: Richard St. John
URL: https://www.ted.com/talks/richard_st_john_s_8_secrets_of_success
GENERAL PURPOSE: To Inform
SPECIFIC PURPOSE: To inform the audience how to be successful in their future careers.

REVERSE OUTLINE

- Introduction
  - »» Attention
    - »"This is really a two-hour presentation I give to high school students, cut down to three minutes. And it all started one day on a plane, on my way to TED, seven years ago."
  - »» Central Idea: There are secrets to achieving success.
    - »"And in the seat next to me was a high school student, a teenager, and she came from a really poor family. And she wanted to make something of her life, and she asked me a simple little question. She said, 'What leads to success?'"
  - »» Importance: Success is something we all want.
  - »» Credibility: The speaker demonstrates empathy.
    - »"So I get off the plane, and I come to TED. And I think, jeez, I'm in the middle of a room of successful people! So why don't I ask them what helped them succeed, and pass it on to kids?"
  - »» Preview of Main Points
    - »He indicates that he will elaborate about what he learned from TEDsters.
    - »(VISUAL) "So here we are, seven years, 500 interviews later, and I'm gonna tell you what really leads to success and makes TEDsters tick."
- Body
  - »» Elaboration of Main Points
    - »Passion

199

- * "And the first thing is passion. (VISUAL) Freeman Thomas says, 'I'm driven by my passion.'" (VISUAL) TEDsters do it for love; they don't do it for money.
- * "Carol Coletta says, 'I would pay someone to do what I do.'" And the interesting thing is: if you do it for love, the money comes anyway."

» Work

- * (VISUAL) "Work! Rupert Murdoch said to me, 'It's all hard work. Nothing comes easily. But I have a lot of fun.' Did he say fun? Rupert? Yes! TEDsters do have fun working. And they work hard. I figured, they're not workaholics. They're workafrolics."

» Practice

- * (VISUAL) "Alex Garden says, 'To be successful put your nose down in something and get damn good at it.' (VISUAL) There's no magic; it's practice, practice, practice."

» Focus

- * (VISUAL) "Norman Jewison said to me, 'I think it all has to do with focusing yourself on one thing.'"

» Push

- * (VISUAL) "David Gallo says, 'Push yourself. Physically, mentally, you've gotta push, push, push.' (VISUAL) You gotta push through shyness and self-doubt."
- * "Goldie Hawn says, 'I always had self-doubts. I wasn't good enough; I wasn't smart enough. I didn't think I'd make it.'"
- * (VISUAL) "Now it's not always easy to push yourself, and that's why they invented mothers. Frank Gehry – Frank Gehry said to me, 'My mother pushed me.'"

» Service

- * (VISUAL) "Sherwin Nuland says, 'It was a privilege to serve as a doctor.'"

Appendix C: Analysis of TED.com

* "Now a lot of kids tell me they want to be millionaires. And the first thing I say to them is: 'OK, well you can't serve yourself; (VISUAL) you gotta serve others something of value. Because that's the way people really get rich.'"

»Ideas

* (VISUAL) "TEDster Bill Gates says, 'I had an idea: founding the first micro-computer software company.' I'd say it was a pretty good idea. (VISUAL) And there's no magic to creativity in coming up with ideas—it's just doing some very simple things. And I give lots of evidence."

»Persistence

* (VISUAL) "Joe Kraus says, 'Persistence is the number one reason for our success.' (VISUAL) You gotta persist through failure. You gotta persist through crap! Which of course means Criticism, Rejection, Assholes, and Pressure."

• Conclusion

»» Recap of Main Points: No recap of main points.

»» Restatement of the Central Idea:

»"Or failing that, do the eight things—(VISUAL) and trust me, these are the big eight things that lead to success."

»» Conclusive Statement

»"Thank you TEDsters for all your interviews!"

CONTENT CRITIQUE

Richard St. John did not employ every element of "ideal" speechmaking. He set up the content of his speech in a brief introduction, and jumped right into citing advice that was collected through a series of interviews. This research process resulted in a list of ideas, as opposed to evenly developed main points with transitions between ideas and multiple sources per point. He also had a very brief conclusion that did not fully recap each of the main ideas, and his conclusive statement was not very memorable.

Despite his failure to conform to the formula of basic public speechwriting, Richard St. John's speech was generally effective. He fulfilled his purpose to inform the audience about "secrets" to success gathered from experts in various fields, and did so in a way that was easy for the audience to follow and understand.

DELIVERY CRITIQUE

Richard St. John utilized many aspects of nonverbal delivery to captivate his audience: his tone, rate, pace, and volume kept his audience engaged throughout the entirety of the speech. His eye contact was consistently strong, as were his use of gestures and posture. The one area that might be critiqued was his reliance on visual aids. Often the audience was forced to read the slides for important back information about the speakers that St. John was referencing. If a slide was missed for whatever reason, or was not seen due to a visual impairment, the audience member may become confused or disinterested in following the rest of the content.

Appendix C: Analysis of TED.com

Exercise: Based on the two previous examples (The Clues to a Great Story and Your Body Language Shapes Who You Are) explain how narrative is used to support the central idea of this speech.

Appendix C: Analysis of TED.com

Persuasive TED Talks

Speech Title: "Talk Nerdy to Me"
Speaker: Melissa Marshall
URL: http://www.ted.com/talks/melissa_marshall_talk_nerdy_to_me
General Purpose: Persuasion
Specific Purpose: To persuade (and inform) scientists about why and how to communicate their ideas more simply and clearly.

Reverse Outline

- Introduction
  - »» Attention: "Five years ago, I experienced a bit of what it must have been like to be Alice in Wonderland."
  - »» Central Idea: "I believe the key to opening that door is great communication."
  - »» Importance: "We desperately need great communication from our scientists and engineers in order to change the world."
  - »» Credibility: "Penn State asked me, a communications teacher, to teach a communications class for engineering students." (This was mentioned immediately after the attention statement.)
  - »» Preview: (No preview.)
- Transition 1: "I want to share a few keys on how you can do that to make sure that we can see that your science is sexy and that your engineering is engaging."
- Body
  - »» Main Point 1: "So what?"
    - »"First question to answer for us: so what? Tell us why your science is relevant to us."
  - »» Main Point 2: Be careful of using jargon.
    - »"And when you're describing your science, beware of jargon."
  - »» Main Point 3: Use stories.
    - »"A few things to consider are having examples, stories, and analogies."

»» Main Point 4: Make full use of presentation aids.

»Drop bullet points and "use a single, readable sentence that the audience can key into if they get a bit lost, and then provide visuals which appeal to our other senses and create a deeper sense of understanding of what's being described."

- Transition 2: "So I think these are just a few keys that can help the rest of us to open that door and see the wonderland that is science and engineering."
- Conclusion

»» Recap of Main Points: An equation for good communication.

»"Take your science, subtract your bullet points and your jargon, divide by relevance, meaning share what's relevant to the audience, and multiply it by the passion that you have for this incredible work that you're doing, and that is going to equal incredible interactions that are full of understanding."

»» Restatement of the Central Idea: (There is no restatement of the central idea.)

»» Conclusive Statement: "And so, scientists and engineers, when you've solved this equation, by all means, talk nerdy to me."

CONTENT CRITIQUE

Melissa Marshall uses almost all of the structural devices present in good speechmaking. Only two criteria are missing: (1) preview of main points, and (2) restatement of the central idea. The decision to omit these items was probably a consequence of the speech's conciseness.

Note also how Melissa doesn't just toss out suggestions, she illustrates every point with examples and supporting material. For example, in explaining why scientists should explain why their work is relevant, she uses the following specific example: "Don't just tell me that you study trabeculae, but tell me that you study trabeculae, which is the mesh-like structure of our bones because it's important to understanding and treating osteoporosis."

Melissa also anticipates and accounts for resistance and criticism to her ideas. As she cautions scientists against using their specialized vocabulary (jargon) to present their ideas to non-scientists, but quickly follows up by noting that this is different from "dumbing it down." Further, she supports this idea with a quotation from Albert Einstein who is arguably the most famous scientist of the twentieth century.

Finally, and perhaps most impressive, Melissa uses the model of an equation to present to give us her recap of main points. Not only is this a summary device, but it places the argument and information present in her speech into a form most familiar to those whom she's presenting to.

Delivery Critique

Melissa Marshall's presentation style is exemplary. Notice how posture, gesture, facial expressions, eye contact, chronemics, and proxemics come together to give the appearance of approachability and confidence. Notice specifically her use of facial expressions to convey her emotions and build a rapport with the audience.

Narrative Tools

Notice how at the beginning of her speech, Melissa explicitly uses her experience being asked to teach communication to engineering students as a way of introducing and framing the information that's to come. Further than this, she also uses the well known tale of Alice in Wonderland as a metaphorical device for stating how communication should serve as a pathway to an interesting new world of ideas.

She also endorses the use of stories in speech with her statement: "A few things to consider are having examples, stories, and analogies."

SPEECH TITLE: "How the Worst Moments in our Lives Make Us Who We Are."
SPEAKER: Andrew Solomon
URL: http://www.ted.com/talks/andrew_solomon_how_the_worst_moments_in_our_lives_make_us_who_we_are
GENERAL PURPOSE: Persuasion
SPECIFIC PURPOSE: To persuade (and inform) listeners about the importance of forging meaning and building identity in their lives.

REVERSE OUTLINE

- Introduction
  - »» Attention: Personal statement.
    - »"As a student of adversity, I've been struck over the years by how some people with major challenges seem to draw strength from them, and I've heard the popular wisdom that that has to do with finding meaning."
  - »» Central Idea: Forge meaning. Build Identity.
    - »"After you've forged meaning, you need to incorporate that meaning into a new identity."
  - »» Importance: Implied by the fact that we must all presumably deal with adversity, but the formal statement of importance is absent.
  - »» Credibility: Andrew has experienced adversity.
    - »Examples of mistreatment in second grade, seventh grade, eighth grade, and high school.
  - »» Preview: No preview.
- Body
  - »» Main Point 1: Avoidance and endurance lead to meaning, which leads to identity formation and triumph over adversity.
    - »The story of the rape victim who became a mother
  - »» Main Point 2: The importance of stories.
    - »"When we're ashamed, we can't tell our stories, and stories are the foundation of identity."

» The story of political prisoners in Myanmar

» The story of Dr. Ma Thida

»» Main Point 3: Experiencing prejudice and hatred lead me to forge and build identity.

» The story of "sexual surrogacy therapy"

» The story of the blonde woman from the Deep South

»» Main Point 4: We don't seek painful experiences, we seek identities.

» "We don't seek the painful experiences that hew our identities, but we seek our identities in the wake of painful experiences."

» "We could have been ourselves without our delights, but not without the misfortunes that drive our search for meaning."

»» Main Point 5: Oppression breeds the power to oppose it.

» The story of his research in 1988 on underground artists in the Soviet Union. The tanks turned back in the face of a stirring speech.

» "Russia awakened me to the lemonade notion that oppression breeds the power to oppose it, and I gradually understood that as the cornerstone of identity."

»» Main Point 6: There is a place for the politics of identity when it is used to fight injustice.

» "But properly understood and wisely practiced, identity politics should expand our idea of what it is to be human. Identity itself should be not a smug label or a gold medal but a revolution."

» Statistics: In the Unites States, in 29 states it's still legal to discriminate against LGBT in matters of employment and housing. Twenty-seven African countries have anti-sodomy laws. In Nigeria, homosexuality is punishable by being stoned to death. In Saudi Arabia, two gay men were recently sentenced to 7,000 lashes each, which rendered them both permanently disabled.

»» Main Point 7: Gay rights are not just a matter of marriage rights.

>»Becoming a husband and a father

>»"As a gay father, I can teach them to own what is wrong in their lives, but I believe that if I succeed in sheltering them from adversity, I will have failed as a parent."

»» Main Point 8: Find happiness in the wake of torment.

>»"I tend to find the ecstasy hidden in ordinary joys, because I did not expect those joys to be ordinary to me."

»The story of George's birthday speech

- Conclusion

    »» Recap of Main Points: (There is no recap of main points.)

    »» Restatement of the Central Idea: "Forge meaning. Build identity."

    »» Conclusive Statement: "Forge meaning. Build identity. Forge meaning. Build identity. And then invite the world to share your joy."

CONTENT CRITIQUE

In this presentation, Andrew Solomon demonstrates the fact that not every successful speech follows the prescribed format of "Introduction" (statement of attention, central idea, importance, credibility, preview), "Body" (orderly elaboration of each main point), and "Conclusion" (recap of main points, restatement of the central idea, and conclusive statement). Like the renowned artist, Pablo Picasso, whose knowledge of realism informed his use of abstraction, Andrew Solomon's awareness of speechmaking conventions gave him creative liberty. In short, one must know the rules in order to break them. For the purposes of this course, you should follow the three-part structure described, but also be able to appreciate variations in format innovated by gifted speakers.

In the introductory portion of his speech, Solomon gains credibility by mentioning the books he's written and, perhaps more importantly, describing the personal struggles he experienced growing up. He also alludes to his central idea, "forge meaning, build identity," but does not state it up front. A statement of importance, though implied, is not formally given, and the preview of main points is missing altogether. The "statement of attention" is more of a personal statement describing his interest in the subject more than anything else.

In watching this speech unfold, you will notice that Solomon weaves back and forth between telling stories and offering declarative statements that summarize the wisdom he's speech lacks a "preview of main points" and because Solomon chooses to build thematic connections between topics, choosing to elaborate more on some than others, the list of main points detailed in the outline above is slightly subjective. Other analysts might identify one or two different points or summarize the points in using different terms. The key thing to note is Solomon's strategy of inductively drawing wisdom from stories once they are told or, alternatively, offering a statement and deductively supporting its truth value with stories.

Solomon transitions into the conclusion of his speech using the "pathos" (emotional persuasion) present in the story of his son George's birthday speech. What remains after this is only a reminder of the central idea as it is combined with the conclusive statement.

Delivery Critique

Andrew Solomon's delivery is excellent. The organizational style of his speech would have been disastrous without his expert execution of chronemics (timing), paralanguage (volume and pitch and tone of voice), and proxemics (use of space on the stage). The only feature of delivery that could have used some improvement from a technical perspective was "gestures" (use of arms and hands). Notice that very few gestures were used throughout the speech and the fact that his left hand is often on his hip or in his pocket.

Let's elaborate a bit more on chronemics, paralanguage, and proxemics:

Profound ideas need big spaces, and Solomon's speech is filled with profound ideas which are meant to stay with you and challenge your thinking long after they've been presented. If this speech were rushed, or if he failed to pause and permit complete silence at various junctures, he would have failed in getting his message across to us. His pacing and use of silent pauses also enhances his credibility and provides him with an air of confidence. The pauses and the drawn out sentences are a sign that he takes these ideas seriously and expects the audience to do the same.

Equally important and strongly related to the pacing of this speech is Solomon's vocal inflection or "paralanguage" to convey his ideas. At points he almost seems to intone his ideas with a hypnotic quality intended to resonate in the audience's psyche. This may seem like a trick or gimmick and has the potential to come off awkward sometimes, but done properly as in this example it can have a dramatic effect on the audience.

Finally, even with a massive audience cloaked in dark blue lights, Solomon makes a point to walk the stage and address individually the different sections splayed out before him. With an audience as large as this, individualized eye contact would be fruitless, but it's still critically important to use posture and proxemics to vary your oriëntation and imply an ongoing engagement with different parts of the audience.

Narrative Tools

Stories are a central feature of this speech, and Andrew Solomon makes no secret of this. In his second main point, he even notes that "stories are the foundation of identity."

Consistent with his respect for narrative truths, there are no fewer than eleven stories in his speech, each varying in length and meant to form different rhetorical functions.

Almost at the start of the speech, Solomon provides four brief stories about his experiences in school that are intended to elicit sympathy from the audience and provide a sense of credibility by proving the adversity he had to face growing up. Also near the beginning of the speech, he uses the story of a woman who has been raped and gives birth as an example intended to demonstrate how people forge meaning out of adversity even in the face of the most abhorrent personal tragedies.

Stories of political prisoners in Myanmar and underground artists in Russia pull from faraway corners of the world where Solomon has visited to bring to us the wisdom of the people who lived them firsthand. The former story (Dr. Ma Thida of Myanmar) was meant to demonstrate ongoing awareness of injustice even in the face of victory ("you can forge meaning and build identity and still be mad as hell") and the latter (the story of the Russian tanks) to show that suffering provides the tools of perseverance.

Perhaps the simplest, but also the most moving story used in the speech was of Andrew's four-year-old son, George, whose birthday speech to his father included telling him "if you were little, I'd be your friend." Notice how this reference to childhood friendships harkens back to the story at the beginning of the speech recounting how Andrew was ostracized by a classmate. In so doing, this device at the end of the speech provides a sense of closure through bracketing the speech within a broader narrative about friendship and personal relationships.

Appendix C: Analysis of TED.com

Speech Title: "The Danger of a Single Story"
Speaker: Chimamanda Ngozi Adichie
URL : http://www.ted.com/talks/chimamanda_adichie_the_danger_of_a_single_story
General Purpose: To persuade
Specific Purpose: To persuade the audience of the danger of the "single story."

Reverse Outline

- Introduction
  - »» Attention: Personal statement of identity.
    - »"I'm a storyteller."
  - »» Central Idea: The "single story" is dangerous.
    - »"And I would like to tell you a few personal stories about what I like to call the danger of the single story."
  - »» Importance: This isn't stated directly, but implied based on the presumed danger of the single story.
  - »» Credibility: Personal background information.
    - »"I grew up on a university campus in eastern Nigeria."
    - »"My mother says that I started reading at the age of two, although I think four is probably close to the truth. So I was an early reader, and what I read were British and American children's books."
  - »» Preview: (No preview.)
- Transition 1: First experiences as a writer.
  - »» "All my characters were white and blue-eyed, they played in the snow, they ate apples, and they talked a lot about the weather, how lovely it was that the sun had come out. Now, this despite the fact that I lived in Nigeria. I had never been outside Nigeria. We didn't have snow, we ate mangoes, and we never talked about the weather, because there was no need to."
  - »» "My characters also drank a lot of ginger beer because the characters in the British books I read drank ginger beer. Never mind that I had no idea what ginger beer was. And for many years afterwards, I would have a desperate desire to taste ginger beer. But that is another story."

»» "What this demonstrates, I think, is how impressionable and vulnerable we are in the face of a story, particularly as children."

- Body

    »» Elaboration of Main Point 1: To me, literature had to be foreign.

    » "Because all I had read were books in which characters were foreign, I had become convinced that books by their very nature had to have foreigners in them and had to be about things with which I could not personally identify."

    »» Elaboration of Main Point 2: African books saved me from the "single story."

    » "So what the discovery of African writers did for me was this: It saved me from having a single story of what books are."

    »» Elaboration of Main Point 3: The "single story" of Africa comes from Western literature.

    » The university story: "Years later, I thought about this when I left Nigeria to go to university in the United States. I was 19. My American roommate was shocked by me. She asked where I had learned to speak English so well, and was confused when I said that Nigeria happened to have English as its official language. She asked if she could listen to what she called my 'tribal music,' and was consequently very disappointed when I produced my tape of Mariah Carey. She assumed that I did not know how to use a stove."

    »» Elaboration of Main Point 4: Stories are about power.

    » "Power is the ability not just to tell the story of another person, but to make it the definitive story of that person."

    »» Elaboration of Main Point 5: Single stories are responsible for stereotypes.

    » "The single story creates stereotypes, and the problem with stereotypes is not that they are untrue, but that they are incomplete. They make one story become the only story."

    »» Elaboration of Main Point 6: There are other stories in Africa beyond catastrophe.

- »"Of course, Africa is a continent full of catastrophes: There are immense ones, such as the horrific rapes in Congo and depressing ones, such as the fact that 5,000 people apply for one job vacancy in Nigeria. But there are other stories that are not about catastrophe, and it is very important, it is just as important, to talk about them."

»» Elaboration of Main Point 7: The consequence of the single story is that it robs us of our dignity.

- »"The consequence of the single story is this: It robs people of dignity. It makes our recognition of our equal humanity difficult. It emphasizes how we are different rather than how we are similar."
- »So what if before my Mexican trip I had followed the immigration debate from both sides, the U.S. and the Mexican? What if my mother had told us that Fide's family was poor and hardworking? What if we had an African television network that broadcast diverse African stories all over the world?"

»» Transition 2: Publishing a book in Nigeria

- »"Shortly after he published my first novel I went to a TV station in Lagos to do an interview, and a woman who worked there as a messenger came up to me and said, 'I really liked your novel. I didn't like the ending. Now you must write a sequel, and this is what will happen ...' (Laughter) And she went on to tell me what to write in the sequel. I was not only charmed, I was very moved. Here was a woman, part of the ordinary masses of Nigerians, who were not supposed to be readers. She had not only read the book, but she had taken ownership of it and felt justified in telling me what to write in the sequel."

• Conclusion

»» Recap of Main Points: What if?

- »"Now, what if my roommate knew about my friend Fumi Onda, a fearless woman who hosts a TV show in Lagos, and is determined to tell the stories that we prefer to forget? What if my roommate knew about the heart procedure that was performed in the Lagos hospital last week? What if my roommate knew about contemporary Nigerian music, talented people singing in English and Pidgin, and Igbo and Yoruba and Ijo, mixing influences from Jay-Z to Fela to Bob Marley to their grandfathers. What if my roommate knew about the female lawyer who recently went to court in Nigeria to challenge a ridiculous law that required women to get their husband's consent before renewing their passports? What if my roommate knew about Nollywood, full of innovative people making films despite great technical odds, films so popular that they really are the best example of Nigerians consuming what they produce? What if my roommate knew about my wonderfully ambitious hair braider, who has just started her own business selling hair extensions? Or about the millions of other Nigerians who start businesses and sometimes fail, but continue to nurse ambition?"

»» Restatement of the Central Idea: (The central idea is not restated.)

»» Conclusive Statement: "When we reject the single story…"

> »"I would like to end with this thought: That when we reject the single story, when we realize that there is never a single story about any place, we regain a kind of paradise."

CONTENT CRITIQUE

Chimamanda Ngozi Adichie's speech is structured around stories and the truths that she draws from them.

In the introduction of her speech, Adichie introduces herself as a storyteller and talks about her own personal history as a girl growing up in Nigeria and as a young storyteller. This self-disclosure helps us to form a connection and identification with her. It also enhances her credibility and provides evidence of her positive "ethos" to the audience. The central idea is clearly stated and the importance of her speech is strongly implied.

The body of the speech is composed of seven main points which are easily identifiable as declarative statements (statements that propose a fact to the audience). (1) To her, literature had to be foreign, (2) African books saved her from the single story, (3) The single story of Africa comes from Western literature, (4) Stories are about power, (5) Single stories are responsible for stereotypes, (6) There are other stories in Africa beyond catastrophe, and (7) The single story robs us of our dignity. Notice carefully how this progression weaves together her personal experience into a greater narrative about stories, Africa, stereotypes, and power. She starts simple, providing evidence through stories, and builds to more complex and abstract points.

The conclusion is perhaps the most powerful and interesting part of the speech. She uses the question phrase "what if…" repeatedly to reference the stories she's already told and, thereby, allude back to the main points she's made throughout the speech. This approach also utilizes the visualization method of Monroe's Motivated Sequence by asking the audience to imagine a world that acknowledges the diversity of stories and of human experience.

DELIVERY CRITIQUE

Adichie's delivery method is extremely formal. She stands behind a podium and makes only minimal use of gestures and no use of proxemics. The cadence of her voice is measured and very purposeful, almost as if the content were read (though it is not). Because she's speaking to a larger audience than a conventional classroom, this style is more appropriate. Furthermore, like an artist, a speaker must find his or her own style of speaking once they have familiarized themselves with all the techniques and conventions of their craft. So, as a professional speaker, the fact that Adichie doesn't use proxemics or extensive gestures of regulation is not necessarily a deficit, but a choice related to personal style. That said, for a smaller group of listeners, it would be more appropriate to step out from behind the podium, use more gestures, and make liberal use of individualized eye contact.

In terms of vocalization, Adichie makes maximum use of paralanguage and chronemics. Her speech is easily comprehensible and simple to follow because we follow the rhythm of her pauses and connect to the rise and fall of her voice, which in part reinforces the verbal content. For example, questioning statements (like "what if ") rise in pitch and declarative statements (as in the main points) fall in pitch.

NARRATIVE TOOLS

Not surprisingly, as a storyteller giving a speech about "the danger of the single story," Adichie makes extensive use of narrative in her speech. In fact, as mentioned earlier, she uses stories as evidence to illustrate her seven main points so that they resonate more strongly with listeners. For example, the story about her family's servant (Fide) is intended to illustrate in very basic introductory terms what the "single story" is all about. She moves from there to her own University experience to describe how the narratives about Africa directly impacted her own personal relationships in America, and how Africa is generally understood by Europe and the United States.

She even uses the story of her visit to Mexico from the United States to reveal her own vulnerability to the lure of the single story and demonstrate with that how seductive it can be.

Transitions represent another way Adichie uses stories as a narrative tool within her speech. The second transition, meant to take the listener out of the body of the speech and into the conclusion is composed of a brief illustration (short story) of a conversation she had with one of her readers. She used the story not only to illustrate the fact that Nigeria was eager to consume its own indigenous literature, but as a way of recapping of her main points and asking the audience to imagine "what if " multiple narratives replaced master narratives.